AWS Certified Cloud Practitioner Practice Exam/Questions

Introduction

Certification is becoming very important in this highly competitive environment. In order to stand out of the crowd, it is highly necessary to grow our skills, get updated and become a unique and demanding professional. This will make us a more preferable candidate among many others. Cloud is the Future of business technology. Now a day's cloud computing is the technology that every business wants. AWS is the God of Cloud. AWS is having growth more than 10 times compared to other players in cloud computing industry. To improve your expertise in cloud computing field AWS certification is best. AWS Certified Cloud Practitioner is the first step to achieving the Professional certification. AWS certified are high on demand and earning a huge amount by acquiring demanded skills. According to this year's salary survey responses, each of the five AWS certifications available report an average salary of more than $100,000 (the average among them all is $125,591).

In this book we have provided 300 practice questions for AWS Certified Cloud Practitioner certification. These questions were framed and reviewed by experts who have great knowledge and experience in AWS Cloud Computing field. Candidates who prepare themselves from this book will gain complete knowledge and confidence about this field. 100% Pass in the examination is assured. We have given certain repeated questions in the book which are considered important by experts. You can easily become an AWS Certified Cloud Practitioner by getting trained using this book. We have also provided the explanation for every answer to make you thorough with all the concepts.

We have taken extreme care in preparing the practice questions for this book. This book was published after being reviewed by experts in many stages. In any case if you find some corrections to be made in the book please feel free to mail us at care@bigbangtechno.in . Our experts will validate it and make the corresponding changes. After the changes are made, we will publish your name with a 'Vote of Thanks' in Amazon Kindle Book Publish website.

We have written this book with the aim of giving the best set of questions to our readers, so that you crack the exam with at most ease. For this, our team has put in their maximum effort and care in framing the questions and explanations. We hope you will be satisfied with this book. If you feel this book has helped you in some way for your preparation, please rate us 5 star in Amazon Kindle. It will be a great moral support to us and will help us to improve the quality of the book in the forthcoming editions. Thanks for considering this book. All the best for your certification. Our prayers for your success in the exam.

Question with Answers

1. To reduce the likelihood of failure, which of the following does AWS perform on your behalf for EBS volumes?

A. Replication of the volume in multiple Availability Zones

B. Replication of the volume in the same Availability Zone

C. Replication of the volume across globe

D. No control over the physical infrastructure

Answer: B

Official Explanation:

Amazon Elastic Block Store (Amazon EBS) provides persistent block storage volumes for use with Amazon EC2 instances in the AWS Cloud. Each Amazon EBS volume is automatically replicated within its Availability Zone to protect you from component failure, offering high availability and durability. Amazon EBS volumes offer the consistent and low-latency performance needed to run your workloads. With Amazon EBS, you can scale your usage up or down within minutes – all while paying a low price for only what you provision.

Amazon EBS is designed for application workloads that benefit from fine tuning for performance, cost and capacity. Typical use cases include Big Data analytics engines (like the Hadoop/HDFS ecosystem and Amazon EMR clusters), relational and NoSQL databases (like Microsoft SQL Server and MySQL or Cassandra and MongoDB), stream and log processing applications (like Kafka and Splunk), and data warehousing applications (like Vertica and Teradata).

Read More From URL: https://aws.amazon.com/ebs/

2. If you want to monitor the CPU utilization of an EC2 resource in AWS , which of the below services can help you in this regard?

A. AWS Cloudwatch

B. AWS Inspector

C. AWS 3

D. AWS User

ANSWER: A

OFFICIAL EXPLANATION:

WHAT IS A CLOUDWATCH?

Amazon CloudWatch is a monitoring and management service built for developers, system operators, site reliability engineers (SRE), and IT managers. CloudWatch provides you with data and actionable insights to monitor your applications, understand and respond to system-wide performance changes, optimize resource utilization, and get a unified view of operational health. CloudWatch collects monitoring and operational data in the form of logs, metrics, and events, providing you with a unified view of AWS resources, applications and services that run on AWS, and on-premises servers. You can use CloudWatch to set high resolution alarms, visualize logs and metrics side by side, take automated actions, troubleshoot issues, and discover insights to optimize your applications, and ensure they are running smoothly. Amazon EC2 sends metrics to Amazon CloudWatch. You can use the AWS Management Console, the AWS CLI, or an API to list the metrics that Amazon EC2 sends to CloudWatch. By default, each data point covers the 5 minutes that follow the start time of activity for the instance. If you've enabled detailed monitoring, each data point covers the next minute of activity from the start time.

Read More From URL:

https://aws.amazon.com/cloudwatch/

https://docs.aws.amazon.com/AWSEC2/latest/UserGuide/viewing_metrics_with_cloudwatch.html

3. A company wants to control access the Amazon EC2 instances which of the following strategies can be used?

A. DynamoDB
B. AWS config
C. AWS Cloud Trail
D. IAM

Answer: D

OFFICIAL EXPLANATION:

Your security credentials identify you to services in AWS and grant you unlimited use of your AWS resources, such as your Amazon EC2 resources. You can use features of Amazon EC2 and AWS Identity and Access Management (IAM) to allow other users, services, and applications to use your Amazon EC2 resources without sharing your security credentials. You can use IAM to control how other users use resources in your AWS account, and you can use security groups to control access to your Amazon EC2 instances. You can choose to allow full use or limited use of your Amazon EC2 resources.

IAM enables you to do the following:

- Create users and groups under your AWS account
- Assign unique security credentials to each user under your AWS account
- Control each user's permissions to perform tasks using AWS resources
- Allow the users in another AWS account to share your AWS resources
- Create roles for your AWS account and define the users or services that can assume them
- Use existing identities for your enterprise to grant permissions to perform tasks using AWS resources

Read More From URL:

https://docs.aws.amazon.com/AWSEC2/latest/UserGuide/Using IAM.html

4. When calculating Total Cost of Ownership(TCO) for the AWS Cloud, which factor must be considered?

A. The ability to choose the highest cost vendor

B. The number of users migrated out of AWS

C. The number of servers migrated to AWS

D. The number of users migrated to AWS

Answer: C

OFFICIAL EXPLANATION:

Since EC2 Instances carry a charge when they are running, you need to factor in the number of servers that need to be migrated to AWS.

Read More From URL:

https://aws.amazon.com/blogs/aws/the-new-aws-tco-calculator/

5. The correct statement about NoSQL and SQL is ?

A. NoSQL and SQL support BCID properties.

B. NoSQL and SQL handle transactions.

C. NoSQL and SQL are relational databases.

D. NoSQL and SQL do not handle transactions

Answer: B

OFFICIAL EXPLANATION:

Amazon Web Services offers you the flexibility to run Microsoft SQL Server for as much or as little time as you need and select from a number of versions and editions. SQL Server on Amazon Elastic Compute Cloud (Amazon EC2) and Amazon Elastic Block Store (Amazon EBS) gives you complete control over every setting, just like when it's installed on-premises. Amazon Relational Database Service (Amazon RDS) is a fully managed service that takes care of all the maintenance, backups, and patching for you.

NoSQL databases are purpose built for specific data models and have flexible schemas for building modern applications. NoSQL databases are widely recognized for their ease of development, functionality, and performance at scale. They use a variety of data models, including document, graph, key-value, in-memory, and search.

Read More From URL:

https://aws.amazon.com/sql/

https://aws.amazon.com/nosql/

6. The service which is not a part of the Cloud Computing models is?

A. Hardware as a Service (HaaS)
B. Software as a Service (SaaS)
C. Performance as a Service (PaaS)
D. AWS Server Union Service(AsuS)

Answer: A

OFFICIAL EXPLANATION:

Cloud computing is providing developers and IT departments with the ability to focus on what matters most and avoid undifferentiated work like procurement, maintenance, and capacity planning. As cloud computing has grown in popularity, several different models and deployment strategies have emerged to help meet specific needs of different users. Each type of cloud service, and deployment method, provides you with different levels of control, flexibility, and management. Understanding the differences between Infrastructure as a Service, Platform as a Service, and Software as a Service, as well as what deployment strategies you can use, can help you decide what set of services is right for your needs.

Read More From URL:

https://aws.amazon.com/types-of-cloud-computing/

7. ABC company wants infrastructure security optimization recommendations, which of the following helps them?

A. Partial upfront reserved instances

B. Dedicated Instances

C. On Demand Instances

D. AWS Trusted Advisor

Answer: D

OFFICIAL EXPLANATION:

The AWS documentation mentions the following An online resource to help you reduce cost, increase performance, and improve security by optimizing your AWS environment, Trusted Advisor provides real time guidance to help you provision your resources following AWS best practices For more information on the AWS Trusted Advisor. AWS Trusted Advisor is an online tool that provides you real time guidance to help you provision your resources following AWS best practices.

Whether establishing new workflows, developing applications, or as part of ongoing improvement, take advantage of the recommendations provided by Trusted Advisor on a regular basis to help keep your solutions provisioned optimally.

Read More From URL:

https://aws.amazon.com/premiumsupport/trustedadvisor/

8. A company wants access to all the checks in the Trusted Advisor Service, how can they do it ? Choose two options.

A. Business

B. Enterprise

C. Account

D. Department

Answer: A and B

OFFICIAL EXPLANATION:

Full Trusted Advisor Benefits

Business Support and Enterprise Support customers get access to the full set of Trusted Advisor checks and recommendations. These help optimize your entire AWS infrastructure, to increase security and performance, reduce your overall costs, and monitor service limits. Additional benefits include:

Notifications: Stay up-to-date with your AWS resource deployment with weekly updates, plus create alerts and automate actions with Amazon CloudWatch.

Programmatic access: Retrieve and refresh Trusted Advisor results programmatically using AWS Support API.

Read More From URL:

https://aws.amazon.com/premiumsupport/technology/trusted-advisor/

9. Multitech, a small company with huge clientele was facing a storage crunch and it wants the resources to be connected to the Internet. What is the ideal solution?

A. Private Subnets

B. Public Subnets

C. Amazon Ec2

D. Hybrid subnets

Answer: B

OFFICIAL EXPLANATION:

A highly available architecture that spans three Availability Zones.

A VPC configured with public and private subnets according to AWS best practices, to provide you with your own virtual network on AWS.

In the public subnets:
Managed NAT gateways to allow outbound internet access for resources in the private subnets.

Two Network Load Balancers to provide Elastic Load Balancing (ELB). There is one load balancer (master ELB) for the master nodes and another (proxy ELB) for the proxy nodes in the private subnets. The load balancers are placed in the public subnets in each of the chosen Availability Zones. Access to cluster administration is limited to the public ports via master node ELB. Access to applications is limited to HTTP/HTTPS via proxy node ELB.

A boot node in one public subnet for command-line cluster administration tasks.

Public Subnets are ideal in an environment where the resources are required to be connected to the Internet.

10. A company's application needs an uptime of at least 99.5%. The deployment strategies they should use is?

A. Establishing the application across multiple networks

B. Deploying the application across same region

C. Deploying the application across multiple Regions

D. Deploying the application across same subnets

Answer: C

OFFICIAL EXPLANATION:

- An AWS account provides multiple Regions so that you can launch Amazon EC2 instances in locations that meet your requirements. For example, you might want to launch instances in Europe to be closer to your European customers or to meet legal requirements.

- An AWS GovCloud (US-West) account provides access to the AWS GovCloud (US-West) Region only. For more information, see AWS GovCloud (US-West) Region.

- An Amazon AWS (China) account provides access to the Beijing and Ningxia Regions only. For more information, see AWS in China.

Read More From URL:

https://docs.aws.amazon.com/AWSEC2/latest/UserGuide/using-regions-availability-zones.html

11. To register a new domain name with AWS, which service can an administrator use?

A. Amazon CLI

B. Amazon Cloud Watch

C. AWS Security groups

D. Amazon Route 53

Answer: D

OFFICIAL EXPLANATION:

Route53 allows for registration of new domain names in AWS The AWS Documentation additionally mentions the following Amazon Route 53 is a highly available and scalable cloud Domain Name System (DNS) web service. It is designed to give developers and businesses an extremely reliable and cost effective way to route end users to Internet applications by translating names like www.example.com into the numeric. IP addresses like 192.0.2.1 that computers use to connect to each other. Amazon Route 53 is fully compliant with IPv6 as well.

Read More From URL:

https://aws.amazon.com/route53/

12. A company wants to monitor all events in their AWS account, in such a case which of the following can help them out ?

A. AWS S3

B. AWS CloudTrail

C. AWS TCO

D. AWS Trusted advisor

Answer: B

OFFICIAL EXPLANATION:

AWS Secrets Manager is integrated with AWS CloudTrail, a service that provides a record of actions taken by a user, role or an AWS service in Secrets Manager. CloudTrail captures all API calls for Secrets Manager as events, including calls from the Secrets Manager console and from code calls to the Secrets Manager APIs. If you create a trail, you can enable continuous delivery of CloudTrail events to an Amazon S3 bucket, including events for Secrets Manager. If you don't configure a trail, you can still view the most recent events in the CloudTrail console in **Event history**.

Using the information collected by CloudTrail, you can determine the request that was made to Secrets Manager the IP address from which the request was made, who made the request, when it was made, and additional details.

Read More From URL:

https://docs.aws.amazon.com/secretsmanager/latest/userguide/monitoring.html

13. XYZ PVT Ltd **wants** to retain application availability, which choice would you prefer?

A. Security Groups
B. Amazon VPC
C. Hybrid cloud
D. Public Subnets

Answer: A

OFFICIAL EXPLANATION:

A *security group* acts as a virtual firewall that controls the traffic for one or more instances. When you launch an instance, you can specify one or more security groups; otherwise, we use the default security group. You can add rules to each security group that allow traffic to or from its associated instances. You can modify the rules for a security group at any time; the new rules are automatically applied to all instances that are associated with the security group. When we decide whether to allow traffic to reach an instance, we evaluate all the rules from all the security groups that are associated with the instance.

Read More From URL:

https://docs.aws.amazon.com/AWSEC2/latest/UserGuide/using -network-security.html

14. A company wants their own private network in the AWS cloud, which option will they choose?

A. AWS EBS Dashboards
B. AWS VPC.
C. AWS SQS
D. AWS SES

Answer: B

OFFICIAL EXPLANATION:

Amazon Virtual Private Cloud (Amazon VPC) lets you provision a logically isolated section of the AWS Cloud where you can launch AWS resources in a virtual network that you define. You have complete control over your virtual networking environment, including selection of your own IP address range, creation of subnets, and configuration of route tables and network gateways.

You can use both IPv4 and IPv6 in your VPC for secure and easy access to resources and applications.

Read More From URL:

https://aws.amazon.com/vpc/

15. Choose the advantage of having AWS Cloud services accessible through Application Programming Interface (API)?

A. Customer –owned, on –premises infrastructure becomes programmable.

B. Cloud resources cannot be managed programmatically

C. All application testing is not managed by EC 2

D. Cloud resources can be managed programmatically

Answer: D

OFFICIAL EXPLANATION:

It allows developers to easily work with the various AWS resources programmatically For more information on the various programming tools available for AWS. The AWS SDK for .NET provides the AWS Resource APIs for .NET. These resource APIs provide a resource-level programming model that enables you to write code to work more directly with resources that are managed by AWS services. A resource is a logical object that is exposed by an AWS service's APIs. For example, AWS Identity and Access

Management (IAM) exposes users and groups as resources that can be programmatically accessed more directly by these resource APIs than by other means.

Read More From URL:

https://docs.aws.amazon.com/sdk-for-net/v2/developer-guide/resource-level-apis-intro.html

16. You want to secure EC2 Instances, which of the following will be useful to you?

A. AWS Config
B. EC2 Groups
C. Security Groups
D. AWS Cloudformation

Answer: C
OFFICIAL EXPLANATION:

A *security group* acts as a virtual firewall that controls the traffic for one or more instances. When you launch an instance, you can specify one or more security groups; otherwise, we use the default security group. You can add rules to each security group that allow traffic to or from its associated instances. You can modify the rules for a security group at any time; the new rules are automatically applied to all instances that are associated with the security group. When we decide whether to allow traffic to reach an instance, we evaluate all the rules from all the security groups that are associated with the instance.

Read More From URL:

https://docs.aws.amazon.com/en_us/AWSEC2/latest/UserGuide/using-network-security.html

17. At the time of disaster what actions will you perform to safeguard your company?

A. Close your datacenter

B. Backup your mission static data

C. Scalable computing capacity routers

D. Launch the replacement compute capacity

Answer: D

OFFICIAL EXPLANATION:

Quickly launch the replacement compute capacity in the cloud for business continuity. After the disaster, restore your data to the data center, and terminate the EC2 instances. **Amazon Elastic Container Service (Amazon ECS)** is a highly scalable, high-performance container orchestration service that supports Docker containers and allows you to easily run and scale containerized applications on AWS. Amazon ECS eliminates the need for you to install and operate your own container orchestration software, manage and scale a cluster of virtual machines, or schedule containers on those virtual machines.

With simple API calls, you can launch and stop Docker-enabled applications, query the complete state of your application, and access many familiar features such as IAM roles, security groups, load balancers, Amazon CloudWatch Events, AWS CloudFormation templates, and AWS CloudTrail logs.

Read More From URL:

https://docs.aws.amazon.com/aws-technical-content/latest/aws-overview/compute-services.html

18. ABC company is planning to develop micro service application consisting of hundreds of services using AWS . It needs a powerful tool for analyzing and debugging. Which tool can be used?

A. AWS X-Ray
B. Amazon EC2
C. Amazon Glacier
D. AWS MFA

Answer: A

OFFICIAL EXPLANATION:

AWS X-Ray helps developers analyze and debug production, distributed applications, such as those built using a microservices architecture. With X-Ray, you can understand how your application and its underlying services are performing to identify and troubleshoot the root cause of performance issues and errors. X-Ray provides an end-to-end view of requests as they travel through your application, and shows a map of your application's underlying components. You can use X-Ray to analyze both applications in development and in production, from simple three-tier applications to complex microservices applications consisting of thousands of services.

Read More From URL:

https://aws.amazon.com/xray/

19. What justifies the statement "design for failure and nothing will fail"?

A. Deploying an application in multiple Availability Zones

B. Creating the cost-effective solution

C. Removing an elastic load balancer in front of a single Amazon Elastic Compute Cloud (Amazon EC2) instance

D. Deploying an application in unique Availability Zone.

Answer: A

OFFICIAL EXPLANATION:

Each AZ is a set of one or more data centers. By deploying your AWS resources to multiple Availability zones, you are designing with failure So if one AZ were to go down, the other AZ's would still be up and running and hence your application would be more fault tolerant.

Read More From URL:

http://docs.aws.amazon.com/AmazonRDS/latest/UserGuide/Concepts.RegionsAndAvailabilityZones.html

20. A company wants to distribute load across multiple EC2 Instances, how can they do it?

A. AWS SQS

B. AWS HDK

C. AWS SDK

D. AWS Elastic Load Balancer

Answer: D

OFFICIAL EXPLANATION:

Elastic Load Balancing automatically distributes incoming application traffic across multiple targets, such as Amazon EC2 instances, containers, IP addresses, and Lambda functions. It can handle the varying load of your application traffic in a single Availability Zone or across multiple Availability Zones. Elastic Load Balancing offers three types of load balancers that all feature the high availability, automatic scaling, and robust security necessary to make your applications fault tolerant.

Read More From URL:

https://aws.amazon.com/elasticloadbalancing/

21. XYZ company wants instance types for high-performance databases, genome analysis, Microsoft SharePoint, distributed caches, and in-memory analytics. Identify the best option.

A. Memory Optimized

B. Hardware Optimized

C. Workloads on mini databases

D. Software optimized Instances

Answer: A

OFFICIAL EXPLANATION:

Memory optimized instance types contains only R3 instances. These instances are optimized to run memory-intensive programs such as high performance databases, genome analysis, Microsoft SharePoint, distributed caches, and in-memory analytics. Amazon EC2 provides a wide selection of instance types optimized to fit different use cases. Instance types comprise varying combinations of CPU, memory, storage, and networking capacity and give you the flexibility to choose the appropriate mix of resources for your applications. Each instance type includes one or more instance sizes, allowing you to scale your resources to the requirements of your target workload.

Read More From URL:

https://aws.amazon.com/ec2/instance-types/

22. An organization which has 500 employees wants to set up AWS access for each department. Which one is a possible solution?

A. Create IAM roles based on the permission and assign users to each role

B. Create IAM groups based on the problems and don't assign IAM users to the individuals.

C. It is possible to manage more than 1000 IAM users with AWS

D. Create IAM groups based on the permission and assign IAM users to the groups

Answer: D

OFFICIAL EXPLANATION:

Create to provide authentication for people and processes in your AWS account. This section also describes IAM *groups*, which are collections of IAM users that you can manage as a unit. Identities represent the user, and can be authenticated and then authorized to perform actions in AWS. Each of these can be associated with one or more policies to determine what actions a user, role, or member of a group can do with which AWS resources and under what conditions.

Read More From URL:

https://docs.aws.amazon.com/IAM/latest/UserGuide/id.html

23. ABC Infotech wants to automate infrastructure provisioning

and administrative tasks for an analytical data warehouse. Which option can help them?

A. Amazon ElastiCache

B. Amazon StaticDB

C. Amazon Redshift

D. AWS X-Ray

Answer: C

OFFICIAL EXPLANATION:

The AWS documentation mentions the following Amazon Redshift is a fully managed, petabyte-scale data warehouse service in the cloud .You can start with just a few hundred gigabytes of data and scale to a petabyte or more. This enables you to use your data to acquire new insights for your business and customers.

Read More From URL:

http://docs.aws.amazon.com/redshift/latest/mgmt/welcome.html

24. To host an application on an EC2 instance that will be used for a minimum of a year, which of the following would be the most cost-effective option?

A. C3

B. Reserved Instances

C. Dedicated Instances

D. Host

Answer: B

OFFICIAL EXPLANATION:

Reserved Instances provide you with a significant discount compared to On-Demand Instance pricing. Reserved Instances are not physical instances, but rather a billing discount applied to the use of On-Demand Instances in your account. These On-Demand Instances must match certain attributes in order to benefit from the billing discount.

Read More From URL:

https://docs.aws.amazon.com/AWSEC2/latest/UserGuide/ec2-reserved-instances.html

25. Your organization wants to use high frequency processors, which instance type will you prefer?

A. Dedicated

B. M2

C. C3   (Compute?)

D. On spot

Answer: C

OFFICIAL EXPLANATION:

The C3 instance type offers high frequency processors for enhanced networking, clustering, and instance storage. The EC2 team took a look back and found that growth in C3 usage to date has been higher than they have seen for any other newly introduced instance type.

Read More From URL:

https://aws.amazon.com/blogs/aws/c3-instance-update/

26. The Shared Security Model gives?

A. Securing corner locations

B. Managing AWS Identity and Access Management (IAM)

C. AWS management console

D. Securing user accounts

Answer: B

OFFICIAL EXPLANATION:

The responsibility of managing the various permissions of users and the roles and permission is with the AWS customer. AWS Identity and Access Management (IAM) is a web service that helps you securely control access to AWS resources. You use IAM to control who is authenticated (signed in) and authorized (has permissions) to use resources.

When you first create an AWS account, you begin with a single sign-in identity that has complete access to all AWS services and resources in the account. This identity is called the AWS account *root user* and is accessed by signing in with the email address and password that you used to create the account. We strongly recommend that you **do not use the root user for your everyday tasks**, even the administrative ones. Instead, adhere to the best practice of using the root user only to create your first IAM user. Then securely lock away the root user credentials and use them to perform only a few account and service management tasks.

Read More From URL:

https://aws.amazon.com/compliance/shared-responsibility-model/

27. A company wants to store a large quantity of archive documents, which of the following storage solutions in AWS will be best suited?

A. AWS Glacier
B. AWS Policies
C. Amazon SQS
D. Amazon Glacier

Answer: D

OFFICIAL EXPLANATION:

Amazon S3 Glacier is a secure, durable, and extremely low-cost cloud storage service for data archiving and long-term backup. It is designed to deliver 99.999999999% durability, and provides comprehensive security and compliance capabilities that can help meet even the most stringent regulatory requirements. Amazon S3

Glacier provides query-in-place functionality, allowing you to run powerful analytics directly on your archive data at rest. Customers can store data for as little as $0.004 per gigabyte per month, a significant savings compared to on-premises solutions. To keep costs low yet suitable for varying retrieval needs, Amazon S3 Glacier provides three options for access to archives, from a few minutes to several hours.

Read More From URL:

https://aws.amazon.com/glacier/

28. Amy wants to use the highest performing processor with the lowest price in Amazon EC2. What should she choose?

A. T3

B. M1

C. C4

D. M2

Answer: C

OFFICIAL EXPLANATION:

The C4 instance type offers the highest performing processors at the lowest price in Amazon EC2. Examples include, C4 dot large, and C4 dot 8xlarge. C4 instances are optimized for compute-intensive workloads and deliver very cost-effective high performance at a low price per compute ratio.

Features:

- High frequency Intel Xeon E5-2666 v3 (Haswell) processors optimized specifically for EC2

- Default EBS-optimized for increased storage performance at no additional cost

- Higher networking performance with Enhanced Networking supporting Intel 82599 VF

- Requires Amazon VPC, Amazon EBS and 64-bit HVM AMIs

Read More From URL:

https://aws.amazon.com/ec2/instance-types/

29. One of your major concerns is Internet attacks such as DDos attacks while hosting an application in AWS. Choose 2 answers of overcoming this attacks.

A. AWS MFA

B. AWS Shield

C. CloudFront

D. AWS EBS Snapshots

Answers: B C

OFFICIAL EXPLANATION:

Automated mitigation techniques are built-into AWS Shield Standard, giving you protection against common, most frequently occurring infrastructure attacks. Automatic mitigations are applied inline to your applications so there is no latency impact. AWS Shield Standard uses several techniques like deterministic packet filtering, and priority based traffic shaping to automatically mitigate attacks without impact to your applications. You can also mitigate application layer DDoS attacks by writing rules using AWS WAF. With AWS WAF you only pay for what you use. When you use AWS Shield Standard with Amazon CloudFront and Amazon Route 53, you receive comprehensive availability protection against all known infrastructure (Layer 3 and 4) attacks.

Read More From URL:

https://aws.amazon.com/shield/features/

30. Consider you want more detail about Amazon Elastic Compute Cloud (Amazon EC2) billing activity that took place 3 month ago, where will you check?

A. AWS Cost and Usage reports

B. Amazon TCO

C. AWS CLI

D. AWS Cloud

Answer: A

OFFICIAL EXPLANATION:

The AWS documentation mentions the following on AWS Cost Reports Cost Explorer is a free tool that you can use to view your costs. You can view data up to the last 13 months, forecast how much you are likely to spend for the next three months, and get recommendations for what Reserved Instances to purchase

Read More From URL:

http://docs.aws.amazon.com/awsaccountbilling/latest/aboutv2/cost-explorer-what-is.html

31. A company wants to send alerts based on Amazon CloudWatch alarms. How can they do it?

A. AWS EBS Volumes

B. AWS SBS

C. AWS TCO

D. Amazon SNS

Answer: D

OFFICIAL EXPLANATION:

Alarms invoke actions for sustained state changes only. CloudWatch alarms do not invoke actions simply because they are in a particular state, the state must have changed and been maintained for a specified number of periods.

After an alarm invokes an action due to a change in state, its subsequent behavior depends on the type of action that you have associated with the alarm. For Amazon EC2 Auto Scaling actions, the alarm continues to invoke the action for every period that the alarm remains in the new state. For Amazon SNS notifications, no additional actions are invoked.

Read More From URL:

https://docs.aws.amazon.com/AmazonCloudWatch/latest/monit
oring/AlarmThatSendsEmail.html

32. Daniel wants to store his website data and also needs a user-
friendly interface. How will Daniel fulfill his demand?

A. Amazon CloudFormation

B. Amazon S3

C. Amazon Cloud9

D. AWS EC2 Dashboard

Answer: B

OFFICIAL EXPLANATION:

Amazon S3 provides safe and secure object storage to developers.
It has a user-friendly interface that helps store and access any
amount of data any time. Amazon Simple Storage Service (Amazon
S3) is an object storage service that offers industry-leading
scalability, data availability, security, and performance. This means
customers of all sizes and industries can use it to store and protect
any amount of data for a range of use cases, such as websites,
mobile applications, backup and restore, archive, enterprise
applications, IoT devices, and big data analytics. Amazon S3
provides easy-to-use management features so you can organize
your data and configure finely-tuned access controls to meet your
specific business, organizational, and compliance requirements.
Amazon S3 is designed for 99.999999999% (11 9's) of durability,

and stores data for millions of applications for companies all around the world.

Read More From URL:

https://aws.amazon.com/s3/

33. If you want high availability and automated backups to your application that has "Net layer" which connects to a MySQL database, which Database do you prefer?

A. An EC2 instance with SQL installed

B. An EC2 with Microsoft SQL installed

C. Aurora

D. An EC2 instance with S3 installed

Answer: C

OFFICIAL EXPLANATION:

Amazon Aurora is a MySQL and PostgreSQL-compatible relational database built for the cloud, that combines the performance and availability of traditional enterprise databases with the simplicity and cost-effectiveness of open source databases.

Amazon Aurora is up to five times faster than standard MySQL databases and three times faster than standard PostgreSQL databases. It provides the security, availability, and reliability of commercial databases at 1/10th the cost. Amazon Aurora is fully managed by Amazon Relational Database Service (RDS), which automates time-consuming administration tasks like hardware provisioning, database setup, patching, and backups.

Read More From URL:

https://aws.amazon.com/rds/aurora/

34. The benefit of running an application across two Availability Zones is?

A. It increases the availability of an application compared to running in a single Availability Zone.

B. It decreases the availability of an application compared to running in a single Availability Zone.

C. It significantly decreases the total cost of ownership versus running in a many Availability Zone.

D. Performance is improved over running in a single Availability Zone.

Answer: A

OFFICIAL EXPLANATION:

Each AZ is a set of one or more data centers. By deploying your AWS resources to multiple Availability zones , you are designing with failure with min D. So if one AZ were to go down , the other AZ's would still be up and running and hence your application would be more fault tolerant.

Read More From URL:

http://docs.aws.amazon.com/AmazonRDS/latest/UserGuide/Concepts.RegionsAndAvailabilityZones.html

35. A global Content Delivery Network (CND) service refers to_____
?

A. Amazon SBS

B. Amazon Cloudfront

C. Amazon CloudFormation

D. Amazon EBS Snapshots

Answer: B

OFFICIAL EXPLANATION:

Amazon CloudFront is a fast content delivery network (CDN) service that securely delivers data, videos, applications, and APIs to customers globally with low latency, high transfer speeds, all within a developer-friendly environment. CloudFront is integrated with AWS – both physical locations that are directly connected to the AWS global infrastructure, as well as other AWS services. CloudFront works seamlessly with services including AWS Shield for DDoS mitigation, Amazon S3, Elastic Load Balancing or Amazon EC2 as origins for your applications, and Lambda@Edge to run custom code closer to customers' users and to customize the user experience.

Read More From URL:

https://aws.amazon.com/cloudfront/

36. Which of the following are included in a comprehensive data policy?

A. Wiping, disposing, retention, and storage

B. Disposing and virtualization

C. Retention, storage and virtualization

D. Storage, retention and elasticity

Answer: A

OFFICIAL EXPLANATION:

Building a data lake and making it the centralized repository for assets that were previously duplicated and placed across many siloes of smaller platforms and groups of users requires implementing stringent and fine-grained security and access controls along with methods to protect and manage the data assets. A data lake solution on AWS—with Amazon S3 as its core—provides a robust set of features and services to secure and protect your data against both internal and external threats, even in large, multi-tenant environments. Additionally, innovative Amazon S3 data management features enable automation and scaling of data lake storage management, even when it contains billions of objects and petabytes of data assets.

Securing your data lake begins with implementing very fine-grained controls that allow authorized users to see, access, process, and modify particular assets and ensure that unauthorized users are blocked from taking any actions that would compromise data confidentiality and security. A complicating factor is that access roles may evolve over various stages of a data asset's processing and lifecycle. Fortunately, Amazon has a comprehensive and well-integrated set of security features to secure an Amazon S3-based data lake.

Read More From URL:

https://docs.aws.amazon.com/aws-technical-content/latest/building-data-lakes/securing-protecting-managing-data.html

37. If you want to run a questionnaire application for only one day (without interruptions), which option do you prefer?

A. On-demand instances

B. Partially upfront Reserved instances

C. Full upfront reserved instances

D. Dedicated Instances

Answer: A

OFFICIAL EXPLANATION:

On-Demand Capacity Reservations enable you to reserve capacity for your Amazon EC2 instances in a specific Availability Zone for any duration. This gives you the ability to create and manage capacity reservations independently from the billing discounts offered by Reserved Instances (RI). By creating Capacity Reservations, you ensure that you always have access to EC2 capacity when you need it, for as long as you need it. Capacity Reservations can be created at any time, without entering into a one-year or three-year term commitment, and the capacity is available immediately. When you no longer need the reservation, cancel the Capacity Reservation to stop incurring charges for it.

When you create a Capacity Reservation, you specify the Availability Zone in which you want to reserve the capacity, the number of instances for which you want to reserve capacity, and the instance attributes, including the instance type, tenancy, and platform/OS. Capacity Reservations can only be used by instances that match their attributes. By default, they are automatically used by running instances that match the attributes. If you don't have any running instances that match the attributes of the Capacity Reservation, it remains unused until you launch an instance with matching attributes.

Read More From URL:

https://docs.aws.amazon.com/AWSEC2/latest/UserGuide/ec2-capacity-reservations.html

38. Choose any of the following two security requirements that are managed by AWS customers?

A. Physical security

B. Tertiary security

C. Password Policies

D. User permissions

E. Hardware patching

Answer: C,D

OFFICIAL EXPLANATION:

As per the Shared Responsibility model , the security for users has to be managed by the AWS Customer. Security and Compliance is a shared responsibility between AWS and the customer. This shared model can help relieve customer's operational burden as AWS operates, manages and controls the components from the host operating system and virtualization layer down to the physical security of the facilities in which the service operates. The customer assumes responsibility and management of the guest operating system (including updates and security patches), other associated application software as well as the configuration of the AWS provided security group firewall. Customers should carefully consider the services they choose as their responsibilities vary depending on the services used, the integration of those services into their IT environment, and applicable laws and regulations. The nature of this shared responsibility also provides the flexibility and customer control that permits the deployment. As shown in the chart below, this differentiation of responsibility is commonly referred to as Security "of" the Cloud versus Security "in" the Cloud.

Read More From URL:

https://aws.amazon.com/compliance/shared-responsibility-model/

39. Which of the following in AWS maps to a separate geographic location?

A. AWS CLI

B. AWS Region

C. AWS Control Region

D. AWS Local Availability zone

Answer: B

OFFICIAL EXPLANATION:

The AWS global infrastructure delivers a cloud infrastructure companies can depend on—no matter their size, changing needs, or challenges. The AWS Global Infrastructure is designed and built to deliver the most flexible, reliable, scalable, and secure cloud computing environment with the highest quality global network performance available today. Every component of the AWS infrastructure is design and built for redundancy and reliability, from regions to networking links to load balancers to routers and firmware.

Read More From URL:

https://aws.amazon.com/about-aws/global-infrastructure/

40. CBC company wants to ease the traffic issues in AWS, what option will you prefer them?

A. Amazon Elastic Load Balancing

B. Amazon Cloud9

C. Amazon Management console

D. Amazon CloudFormation

Answer: A

OFFICIAL EXPLANATION:

Elastic Load Balancing, or ELB, service disseminates the network traffic across a group of virtual servers.

Elastic Load Balancing automatically distributes incoming application traffic across multiple targets, such as Amazon EC2 instances, containers, IP addresses, and Lambda functions. It can handle the varying load of your application traffic in a single Availability Zone or across multiple Availability Zones. Elastic Load Balancing offers three types of load balancers that all feature the high availability, automatic scaling, and robust security necessary to make your applications fault tolerant.

Read More From URL:

https://aws.amazon.com/elasticloadbalancing/

41. A company without affecting the functionality of the source database decided to migrate it's Oracle database to AWS . Which service can help them?

A. AWS Database Migration Service
B. Amazon user account
C. AWS Application manager
D. RDS Unique-AZ

Answer: A

OFFICIAL EXPLANATION:

AWS Database Migration Service helps you migrate databases to AWS quickly and securely. The source database remains fully operational during the migration, minimizing downtime to applications that rely on the database. The AWS Database Migration Service can migrate your data to and from most widely used commercial and open-source databases.

AWS Database Migration Service supports homogeneous migrations such as Oracle to Oracle, as well as heterogeneous migrations between different database platforms, such as Oracle or Microsoft SQL Server to Amazon Aurora. With AWS Database Migration Service, you can continuously replicate your data with high availability and consolidate databases into a petabyte-scale data warehouse by streaming data to Amazon Redshift and Amazon S3.

Read More From URL:

https://aws.amazon.com/dms/

42. The cloud architecture principle of elasticity will :

A. Create systems that scale more than the required capacity based on changes in demand

B. Create systems that scale to the required capacity based on change of customers

C. Create systems that scale to the required capacity based on changes in demand

D. Deploy the application across Edge locations

Answer: C

OFFICIAL EXPLANATION:

The concept of Elasticity is the means of an application having the ability to scale up and scale down based on demand . An example of such a service is the Autoscaling service. The elasticity of cloud services is a powerful way to optimize costs. By combining tagging, monitoring, and automation, your organization can match its spending to its needs and put resources where they provide the most value. For more information about elasticity and other cost management topics, see the AWS Billing and Cost Management documentation. Automation tools can help minimize some of the management and administrative tasks associated with an IT deployment. Similar to the benefits from application services, an automated or DevOps approach to your AWS infrastructure will provide scalability and elasticity with minimal manual intervention.

Read More From URL:

https://aws.amazon.com/autoscaling/

43. ABC Multitech is planning to host a development environment on the cloud consisting of EC2 and RDS instances required for 2 months. Which type of instances would you use for this purpose?

A. Determined

B. Dedicated

C. On-Demand

D. Department

Answer: C

OFFICIAL EXPLANATION:

Provide a significant discount compared to running instances On-Demand.

- Can apply to usage across all Availability Zones in an AWS region, or can provide a capacity reservation when assigned to a specific Availability Zone.

- Are offered under three upfront payment options to provide you with payment flexibility at the point of purchase.

- Can be shared between multiple accounts within a consolidated billing family.

Read More From URL:

https://aws.amazon.com/ec2/pricing/reserved-instances/

44. XYZ company wants to use network services that would implement its code from Amazon EC2 instances on the virtual servers. What should the company use?

A. AWS console

B. Amazon EC dashboard

C. manual Scaling Service

D. AWS Lambda

Answer: D

OFFICIAL EXPLANATION:

AWS Lambda service implements the code from Amazon EC2 instances on the virtual servers, in response to a triggered event.

AWS Lambda lets you run code without provisioning or managing servers. You pay only for the compute time you consume - there is no charge when your code is not running.

With Lambda, you can run code for virtually any type of application or backend service - all with zero administration. Just upload your code and Lambda takes care of everything required to run and scale your code with high availability. You can set up your code to automatically trigger from other AWS services or call it directly from any web or mobile app.

Read More From URL:

https://aws.amazon.com/lambda/

45. XYZ company wants object level storage in AWS, which service satisfies the condition ?

A. Amazon EC2

B. Amazon SQS

C. Amazon S3

D. Amazon SES

Answer: C

OFFICIAL EXPLANATION:

Amazon S3 has various features you can use to organize and manage your data in ways that support specific use cases, enable cost efficiencies, enforce security, and meet compliance requirements. Data is stored as objects within resources called "buckets", and a single object can be up to 5 terabytes in size. S3 features include capabilities to append metadata tags to objects, move and store data across the S3 Storage Classes, configure and enforce data access controls, secure data against unauthorized users, run big data analytics, and monitor data at the object and bucket levels.

Read More From URL:

https://aws.amazon.com/s3/features/

46. Amazon Elastic Compute Cloud (Amazon EC2) Spot instances is chosen for which of the following workloads?

A. Workloads where the availability of the Amazon EC2 instances can be flexible

B. Workloads that are only run in the morning and stopped at night

C. Workloads that need to run for long periods of time without interruption

D. Workloads where the availability of the Amazon EC2 instances cannot be flexible.

Answer: A

OFFICIAL EXPLANATION:

The AWS documentation mentions the following Spot Instances are a cost-effective choice if you can be flexible about when your applications run and if your applications can be interrupted. For example, Spot Instances are well-suited for data analysis, batch jobs, background processing, and optional tasks.

Read More From URL:

http://docs.aws.amazon.com/AWSEC2/latest/UserGuide/using-spot-instances.html

47. An application was developed in .NET which works with the S3 buckets in a particular region hosted on an EC2 Instance . You want to ensure that the EC2 Instance has the appropriate access to the S3 buckets. How will you do it?

A. Aurora

B. AWS IAM Roles

C. AWS MFA

D. AWS S3

Answer: B

OFFICIAL EXPLANATION:

IAM role to manage *temporary* credentials for applications that run on an EC2 instance. When you use a role, you don't have to distribute long-term credentials (such as a user name and password or access keys) to an EC2 instance. Instead, the role supplies temporary permissions that applications can use when they make calls to other AWS resources. When you launch an EC2 instance, you specify an IAM role to associate with the instance.

Applications that run on the instance can then use the role-supplied temporary credentials to sign API requests.

Read More From URL:

https://docs.aws.amazon.com/IAM/latest/UserGuide/id_roles_u se_switch-role-ec2.html

48. Choose the most appropriate option to use the DNS Web service?

A. Amazon Route 53 Hosted Zones

B. Manual Scaling Groups

C. Hybrid cloud

D. Private cloud

Answer: A

OFFICIAL EXPLANATION:

Amazon Route 53, a DNS Web service, is scalable, highly available, and a cost-effective medium to direct the visitors to a website, a virtual server, or a load balancer. Amazon Route 53 is a highly available and scalable cloud Domain Name System (DNS) web service. It is designed to give developers and businesses an extremely reliable and cost effective way to route end users to Internet applications by translating names like www.example.com into the numeric IP addresses like 192.0.2.1 that computers use to connect to each other. Amazon Route 53 is fully compliant with IPv6 as well.

Amazon Route 53 effectively connects user requests to infrastructure running in AWS – such as Amazon EC2 instances, Elastic Load Balancing load balancers, or Amazon S3 buckets – and can also be used to route users to infrastructure outside of AWS. You can use Amazon Route 53 to configure DNS health checks to route traffic to healthy endpoints or to independently monitor the health of your application and its endpoints. Amazon Route 53 Traffic Flow makes it easy for you to manage traffic globally through a variety of routing types, including Latency Based Routing, Geo DNS, Geoproximity, and Weighted Round Robin— all of which can be combined with DNS Failover in order to enable a variety of low-latency, fault-tolerant architectures. Using Amazon Route 53 Traffic Flow's simple visual editor, you can easily manage how your end-users are routed to your application's endpoints— whether in a single AWS region or distributed around the globe. Amazon Route 53 also offers Domain Name Registration – you can purchase and manage domain names such as example.com and Amazon Route 53 will automatically configure DNS settings for your domains.

Read More From URL:

https://aws.amazon.com/route53/

49. A product application based company has a DevOps team in its organization and they want to manage infrastructure as code. Which of the following would you suggest for them?

A. Firewall

B. AWS Cloudformation

C. AWS Cloud9

D. Amazon S3

Answer: B

OFFICIAL EXPLANATION:

AWS CloudFormation provides a common language for you to describe and provision all the infrastructure resources in your cloud environment. CloudFormation allows you to use a simple text file to model and provision, in an automated and secure manner, all the resources needed for your applications across all regions and accounts. This file serves as the single source of truth for your cloud environment.

Read More From URL:

https://aws.amazon.com/cloudformation/

50. A user wants to manage services through a web-based user interface, choose the option which will suit him?

A. Amazon CloudFormation

B. AWS CLI

C. AWS Hardware Development Kit (HDK)

D. AWS Management Console

Answer: D

OFFICIAL EXPLANATION:

The AWS Management console allows you to access and manage Amazon Web Services through a simple and intuitive web-based user interface. The AWS Management Console is a web application that comprises and refers to a broad collection of service consoles for managing Amazon Web Services. When you first sign in, you see the console home page. The home page provides access to each service console as well as an intuitive user interface for exploring AWS and getting helpful tips. Among other things, the individual service consoles offer tools for working with Amazon S3 buckets, launching and connecting to Amazon EC2 instances, setting Amazon CloudWatch alarms, and getting information about your account and about billing

Read More From URL:

https://aws.amazon.com/console/

51. Your firm has several independent AWS accounts and linked AWS accounts. What is the best way to manage monthly payment invoices from AWS?

A. AWS cloud formation

B. AWS Management console

C. AWS Consolidated Billing

D. AWS Assorted Billing

Answer: C

OFFICIAL EXPLANATION:

You can use the consolidated billing feature in AWS Organizations to consolidate billing and payment for multiple AWS accounts or multiple Amazon Internet Services Pvt. Ltd (AISPL) accounts. Every organization in AWS Organizations has a *master account* that pays the charges of all the *member accounts*. For more information about organizations, see the AWS Organizations User Guide. For the rest of this guide, the master account is called a payer account, and the member account is called a linked account, even when we talk about organizations.

Read More From URL:

https://docs.aws.amazon.com/awsaccountbilling/latest/aboutv2/consolidated-billing.html

52. Elastic Load Balancer has higher fault-tolerance level. How?

A. Dividing instances into several Availability Zones

B. Launch the replacement compute capacity

C. Multiplying instances into one availability Zones

D. Destroying subnets

Answer: A

OFFICIAL EXPLANATION:

A Load Balancer is responsible for distributing the network traffic across Amazon EC2 instances in different Availability Zones, which enables you to accomplish a higher fault-tolerance level. A load balancer accepts incoming traffic from clients and routes requests to its registered targets (such as EC2 instances) in one or more Availability Zones. The load balancer also monitors the health of its registered targets and ensures that it routes traffic only to healthy targets. When the load balancer detects an unhealthy target, it stops routing traffic to that target, and then resumes routing traffic to that target when it detects that the target is healthy again.

You configure your load balancer to accept incoming traffic by specifying one or more *listeners*. A listener is a process that checks for connection requests. It is configured with a protocol and port number for connections from clients to the load balancer and a protocol and port number for connections from the load balancer to the targets.

Read More From URL:

https://docs.aws.amazon.com/elasticloadbalancing/latest/usergui de/how-elastic-load-balancing-works.html

53. Which of the following is NOT TRUE about its cost, regarding On-Demand instances in AWS?

A. There is no upfront costs for the instance

B. You pay for how much you use.

C. You are charged per hour based on the hourly rate

D. You have to pay the termination fees if you terminate the instance .

Answer: D

OFFICIAL EXPLANATION:

On-Demand instances let you pay for compute capacity by the hour or second (minimum of 60 seconds) with no long-term commitments. This frees you from the costs and complexities of planning, purchasing, and maintaining hardware and transforms what are commonly large fixed costs into much smaller variable costs.

The pricing below includes the cost to run private and public AMIs on the specified operating system ("Windows Usage" prices apply to Windows Server 2003 R2, 2008, 2008 R2, 2012, 2012 R2, and 2016). Amazon also provides you with additional instances for Amazon EC2 running Microsoft Windows with SQL Server, Amazon EC2 running SUSE Linux Enterprise Server, Amazon EC2 running Red Hat Enterprise Linux and Amazon EC2 running IBM that are priced differently.

Read More From URL:

https://aws.amazon.com/ec2/pricing/on-demand/

54. You want to display the distribution of AWS spending, which service will you take use of?

A. AWS EBS Volumes

B. Amazon Policy

C. AWS Cost Explorer

D. AWS SQS

Answer: C

OFFICIAL EXPLANATION:

The AWS Documentation mentions the following Cost Explorer is a free tool that you can use to view your costs. You can view data up to the last 13 months, forecast how much you are likely to spend for the next three months, and get recommendations for what Reserved Instances to purchase. You can use Cost Explorer to see patterns in how much you spend on AWS resources over time, identify areas that need further inquiry, and see trends that you can use to understand your costs. You also can specify time ranges for the data, and view time data by day or by month.

Read More From URL:

http://docs.aws.amazon.com/awsaccountbilling/latest/aboutv2/c ost-explorer-what-is.html

55. For finding information about prohibited actions on AWS infrastructure, where should you go?

A. AWS Cloud9

B. AWS Acceptable USE Policy

C. AWS TCO

D. AWS CLI

Answer: B

OFFICIAL EXPLANATION:

This Acceptable Use Policy (this "Policy") describes prohibited uses of the web services offered by Amazon Web Services, Inc. and its affiliates (the "Services") and the website located at http://aws.amazon.com (the "AWS Site"). The examples described in this Policy are not exhaustive. We may modify this Policy at any time by posting a revised version on the AWS Site. By using the Services or accessing the AWS Site, you agree to the latest version of this Policy. If you violate the Policy or authorize or help others to do so, we may suspend or terminate your use of the

Services.

Read More From URL:

https://aws.amazon.com/aup/

56. Infotech company wants Web services that offer scalable computing capacity servers. What should that company choose?

A. Auto Scaling Groups

B. Amazon EC2

C. Amazon S3

D. Easy Scaling Groups

Answer: B

OFFICIAL EXPLANATION:

Amazon Elastic Compute Cloud (Amazon EC2) is a web service that provides secure, resizable compute capacity in the cloud. It is designed to make web-scale cloud computing easier for developers.

Read More From URL:

https://aws.amazon.com/ec2

57. Adding more hard drives to a storage array is an example of _____ . Upgrading a server with a larger hard drive is an example of _____ .

A. Horizontal Scaling, Vertical Scaling.

B. Vertical Scaling, Vertical Scaling.

C. Vertical Scaling, Horizontal Scaling.

D. Horizontal Scaling, Horizontal Scaling.

Answer: A

OFFICIAL EXPLANATION:

To handle a higher load in your database, you can vertically scale up your master database with a simple push of a button. There are currently over 18 instance sizes that you can choose from when resizing your RDS MySQL, PostgreSQL, MariaDB, Oracle, or Microsoft SQL Server instance. For Amazon Aurora, you have 5 memory-optimized instance sizes to choose from. The wide selection of instance types allows you to choose the best resource and cost for your database server.

Read More From URL:

https://aws.amazon.com/blogs/database/scaling-your-amazon-rds-instance-vertically-and-horizontally/

58. Criozel company wants the AWS Management Console be secured against unauthorized access, what option do you prefer for them?

A. Set up a tertiary password

B. Apply Multi-Factor Authentication (MFA)

C. Request root denied privileges

D. Disable MFA

Answer: B

OFFICIAL EXPLANATION:

The AWS Documentation mentions the following AWS Multi-Factor Authentication (MFA) is a simple best practice that adds an extra layer of protection on top of your user name and password.

Read More From URL:

https://aws.amazon.com/iam/details/mfa/

59. You want a service which is fully managed AWS database service , which one can be made suitable?

A. Amazon NoSQL

B. Amazon DynamoDB

C. MariaDB

D.Microsoft SQL

Answer: B

OFFICIAL EXPLANATION:

Amazon DynamoDB is a NoSQL database that supports key-value and document data models, and enables developers to build modern, serverless applications that can start small and scale globally to support petabytes of data and tens of millions of read and write requests per second. DynamoDB is designed to run high-performance, internet-scale applications that would overburden traditional relational databases.

Read More From URL:

https://aws.amazon.com/dynamodb/features/

60. Choose the uses of T2 instances?

A. Workloads on small databases

B. Batch producing payloads

C. Shares Keywords

D. Launches an Account

Answer: A

OFFICIAL EXPLANATION:

T2 instances are used for workloads on small databases, Web Servers, low-traffic sites, and development environments. T2 instances are a low-cost, general purpose instance type that provides a baseline level of CPU performance with the ability to burst above the baseline when needed. With On-Demand Instance prices starting at $0.0058 per hour, T2 instances are one of the lowest-cost Amazon EC2 instance options and are ideal for a variety of general-purpose applications like micro-services, low-latency interactive applications, small and medium databases, virtual desktops, development, build and stage environments, code repositories, and product prototypes.

Read More From URL:

https://aws.amazon.com/ec2/instance-types/t2/

61. A company wants the user to achieve automated scalability, from which of these services can they get help from?

A. Cloud9

B. Aurora

C. AWS CloudFormation

D. S3

Answer: D

OFFICIAL EXPLANATION:

Amazon Simple Storage Service (Amazon S3) is an object storage service that offers industry-leading scalability, data availability, security, and performance. This means customers of all sizes and industries can use it to store and protect any amount of data for a range of use cases, such as websites, mobile applications, backup and restore, archive, enterprise applications, IoT devices, and big data analytics. Amazon S3 provides easy-to-use management features so you can organize your data and configure finely-tuned access controls to meet your specific business, organizational, and compliance requirements. Amazon S3 is designed for 99.999999999% (11 9's) of durability, and stores data for millions of applications for companies all around the world.

Read More From URL:

https://aws.amazon.com/s3/

63. To turn on Multi-Factor Authentication (MFA), Which AWS Cloud service can be used?

A. AWS EBS Volumes

B. Amazon S3

C. AWS Identity and Access Management (IAM)

D. AWS MFA

Answer: C

OFFICIAL EXPLANATION:

The AWS Documentation mentions the following You can use IAM in the AWS Management Console to enable a virtual MFA device for an IAM user in your account. AWS Multi-Factor Authentication (MFA) is a simple best practice that adds an extra layer of protection on top of your user name and password. With MFA enabled, when a user signs in to an AWS website, they will be prompted for their user name and password (the first factor—what they know), as well as for an authentication response from their AWS MFA device (the second factor—what they have). Taken together, these multiple factors provide increased security for your AWS account settings and resources.You can enable MFA for your AWS account and for individual IAM users you have created under your account. MFA can be also be used to control access to AWS service APIs.

Read More From URL:

http://docs.aws.amazon.com/IAM/latest/UserGuide/id_credenti als_mfa_enable_virtual.html

64. Amazon EC2 supports which of the following platforms?

A. C3 dot 2xlarge and C3 dot 8xlarge

B. EC2 Classic and EC2 VPC

C. D3 dot 16xlarge and D2 dot 8xlarge

D. C3 dot large and D5 dot 32xlarge

Answer: B

OFFICIAL EXPLANATION:

Amazon Virtual Private Cloud (Amazon VPC) enables you to define a virtual network in your own logically isolated area within the AWS cloud, known as a *virtual private cloud (VPC)*. You can launch your Amazon EC2 resources, such as instances, into the subnets of your VPC. Your VPC closely resembles a traditional network that you might operate in your own data center, with the benefits of using scalable infrastructure from AWS. You can configure your VPC; you can select its IP address range, create subnets, and configure route tables, network gateways, and security settings. You can connect instances in your VPC to the internet or to your own data center.When you create your AWS account, we create a *default VPC* for you in each region. A default VPC is a VPC that is already configured and ready for you to use. You can launch instances into your default VPC immediately. Alternatively, you can create your own *nondefault VPC* and configure it as you need.If you created your AWS account before 2013-12-04, you might have support for the EC2-Classic platform in some regions. If you created your AWS account after 2013-12-04, it does not support EC2-Classic, so you must launch your resources in a VPC.

Read More From URL:

https://docs.aws.amazon.com/AWSEC2/latest/UserGuide/using-vpc.html

65. A company wants to display the distribution of AWS spending.

Which tool can be used?

A. AWS Cost Explorer

B. Amazon Policies

C. AWS CLI

D. Amazon DevOps

Answer: A

OFFICIAL EXPLANATION:

AWS Cost Explorer has an easy-to-use interface that lets you visualize, understand, and manage your AWS costs and usage over time. Get started quickly by creating custom reports (including charts and tabular data) that analyze cost and usage data, both at a high level (e.g., total costs and usage across all accounts) and for highly-specific requests (e.g., m2.2xlarge costs within account Y that are tagged "project: secretProject"). Using AWS Cost Explorer, you can dive deeper into your cost and usage data to identify trends, pinpoint cost drivers, and detect anomalies.

Read More From URL:

https://aws.amazon.com/aws-cost-management/aws-cost-explorer/

66. A disaster recovery strategy on AWS should be based on launching infrastructure in a separate:

A. Public Subnet

B. Availability zone

C. AWS corner location

D. AWS Region

Answer: D

OFFICIAL EXPLANATION:

The AWS Documentation mentions the following Businesses are using the AWS cloud to enable faster disaster recovery of their critical IT systems without incurring the infrastructure expense of a second physical site. The AWS cloud supports many popular disaster recovery (DR) architectures from "pilot light" environments that may be suitable for small customer workload data center failures to "hot standby" environments that enable rapid failover at scale. With data centers in Regions all around the world, AWS provides a set of cloud-based disaster recovery services that enable rapid recovery of your IT infrastructure and data.

Read More From URL:

https://aws.amazon.com/disaster-recovery/

67. The feature that does NOT allow to download the AWS Console app.

A. Flipkart app store

B. Blackberry store

C. Google play store

D. Google App store

Answer: B

OFFICIAL EXPLANATION:

The Console Mobile Application allows AWS customers to monitor resources through a dedicated dashboard and view configuration details, metrics, and alarms for select AWS services. The Dashboard provides permitted users with a single view a resource's status, with real-time data on Amazon CloudWatch, Personal Health Dashboard, and AWS Billing and Cost Management. Customers can view ongoing issues and follow through to the relevant CloudWatch alarm screen for a detailed view with graphs and configuration options. In addition, customers can check on the status of specific AWS services, view detailed resource screens, and perform select actions.

Read More From URL:

https://aws.amazon.com/console/mobile/

68. Which of the following AWS services provides infrastructure security optimization recommendations?

A. AWS IAM
B. AWS Cloud9
C. AWS Trusted Advisor
D. Amazon SES

Answer: C

OFFICIAL EXPLANATION:

AWS Trusted Advisor is an online tool that provides you real time guidance to help you provision your resources following AWS best practices.

Whether establishing new workflows, developing applications, or as part of ongoing improvement, take advantage of the recommendations provided by Trusted Advisor on a regular basis to help keep your solutions provisioned optimally.

Read More From URL:

https://aws.amazon.com/premiumsupport/technology/trusted-advisor/

69. When calculating Total Cost of Ownership (TCO) for the AWS Cloud, which of the following is a factor?

A. The number of users migrated out of AWS

B. The number of servers migrated to AWS

C. The number of passwords migrated to AWS

D. The number of keys migrated out of AWS

Answer: B

OFFICIAL EXPLANATION:

Since EC2 Instances carry a charge when they are running, you need to factor in the number of servers that need to be migrated to AWS.

Read More From URL:

https://aws.amazon.com/blogs/aws/the-new-aws-tco-calculator/

70. AWS Import/Export service supports which of the following services?

A. AWS CLI

B. Amazon EC2 Dashboard

C. Amazon Aurora

D. AWS Import/Export Disk

Answer: D

OFFICIAL EXPLANATION:

If you have large amounts of data to load and an Internet connection with limited bandwidth, the time required to prepare and ship a portable storage device to AWS can be a small percentage of the time it would take to transfer your data over the internet. If loading your data over the Internet would take a week or more, you should consider using AWS Import/Export Disk.

Read More From URL:

https://aws.amazon.com/snowball/disk/details/

71. Which of the following included services could assist a company using the Enterprise Support plan, if the company wants a quick and efficient guidance with their billing and account inquiries.?

A. AWS Support Concierge

B. AWS Security groups

C. Aurora

D. Amazon User

Answer: A

OFFICIAL EXPLANATION:

AWS Enterprise Support provides you with concierge-like service where the main focus is helping you achieve your outcomes and find success in the cloud.With Enterprise Support, you get 24x7 technical support from high-quality engineers, tools and technology to automatically manage health of your environment, consultative architectural guidance delivered in the context of your applications and use-cases, and a designated Technical Account Manager (TAM) to coordinate access to proactive / preventative programs and AWS subject matter experts.

Read More From URL:

https://aws.amazon.com/premiumsupport/plans/enterprise/

72.Which AWS service is used as a global content delivery network (CDN) service in AWS?

A. Amazon SQS

B. Amazon Glacier

C. Amazon CloudFront

D. Amazon EBS Snapshots

Answer: C

OFFICIAL EXPLANATION:

The AWS Documentation mentions the following Amazon CloudFront is a web service that gives businesses and web application developers an easy and cost effective way to distribute content with low latency and high data transfer speeds. Like other AWS services, Amazon CloudFront is a self-service, pay-per-use offering, requiring no long term commitments or minimum fees. With CloudFront, your files are delivered to end-users using a global network of edge locations.

Read More From URL:

https://aws.amazon.com/cloudfront/

73. To examine the customer's AWS environment, identify security gaps, and fill them, which tool in AWS can be used ?

A. Trusted Guide
B. Trusted Advisor
C. Trusted Counselor
D. Trusted Controller

Answer: B

74. A part of the Enterprise support plan, Who is the primary point of contact for the ongoing support needs?

A. TSM
B. SQL
C. SBS
D. TAM

Answer: D

OFFICIAL EXPLANATION:

Designated Technical Account Manager (TAM) to proactively monitor your environment and assist with optimization.

Read More From URL:

https://aws.amazon.com/premiumsupport/plans/

75. A fully managed NoSQL database service available with AWS is

A. AWS RDS

B. AWS DynamoDB

C. Microsoft SQL

D. AWS MariaDB

Answer: B

OFFICIAL EXPLANATION:

The AWS Documentation mentions the following Amazon DynamoDB is a fast and flexible NoSQL database service for all applications that need consistent, single-digit millisecond latency at any scale. It is a fully managed cloud database and supports both document and key-value store models. Its flexible data model, reliable performance, and automatiC. scaling of throughput capacity, makes it a great fit for mobile, web, gaming, ad tech, IoT, and many other applications.

Read More From URL:

https://aws.amazon.com/dynamodb/

76. For non-stop monitoring, logging, and auditing of physical access controls, which tool can be used?

A. Physical Security

B. User keyword

C. Local Guidance

D. Tertiary Security

Answer: A

OFFICIAL EXPLANATION:

The AWS team undertakes the key measure for providing non-stop monitoring, logging, and auditing of physical access controls.

Read More From URL:

https://aws.amazon.com/security/

77. NextGen company is trying to organize and import (to AWS) gigabytes of data that are currently structured in JSON-like, name-value documents. What AWS service would best fit your needs?

A. Lambda

B. Policy

C. DynamoDB

D. Sigma

Answer: C

OFFICIAL EXPLANATION:

The AWS Documentation mentions the following Amazon DynamoDB is a fast and flexible NoSQL database service for all applications that need consistent, single-digit millisecond latency at any scale. It is a fully managed cloud database and supports both document and key-value store models. Its flexible data model, reliable performance, and automatiC. scaling of throughput capacity, makes it a great fit for mobile, web, gaming, ad tech, IoT, and many other applications.

Read More From URL:

https://aws.amazon.com/dynamodb/

78. A company wants to store data that is not frequently accessed in a more efficient and cost efficient way. Which is the best solution for this?

A. Amazon Storage Gateway

B. Microsoft SQL

C. Amazon RDS

D. Glacier

Answer: D

OFFICIAL EXPLANATION:

The AWS Documentation mentions the following Amazon Glacier is a secure, durable, and extremely low-cost cloud storage service for data archiving and long-term backup. It is designed to deliver 99.999999999% durability, and provides comprehensive security and compliance capabilities that can help meet even the most stringent regulatory requirements.

Read More From URL:

https://aws.amazon.com/glacier/

79. Choose the option that is a scalable and an economical amalgamation of your office IT and AWS storage infrastructure?

A. AWS MFA

B. AWS EBS Volume

C. Amazon CLI

D. AWS Storage Gateway

Answer: D

OFFICIAL EXPLANATION:

AWS Storage Gateway is a scalable and an economical amalgamation of your office IT and AWS storage infrastructure.

AWS Storage Gateway is a hybrid storage service that enables your on-premises applications to seamlessly use AWS cloud storage. You can use the service for backup and archiving, disaster recovery, cloud data processing, storage tiering, and migration. The service helps you reduce and simplify your datacenter and branch or remote office storage infrastructure. Your applications connect to the service through a virtual machine or hardware gateway appliance using standard storage protocols, such as NFS, SMB and iSCSI. The gateway connects to AWS storage services, such as

Amazon S3, Amazon S3 Glacier, Amazon S3 Glacier Deep Archive, Amazon EBS, and AWS Backup, providing storage for files, volumes, snapshots, and virtual tapes in AWS. The service includes a highly-optimized data transfer mechanism, with bandwidth management, automated network resilience, and efficient data transfer, along with a local cache for low-latency on-premises access to your most active data.

Read More From URL:

https://aws.amazon.com/storagegateway/

80. A company wants to reduce the possibility of failure. What does AWS perform for EBS volumes?

A. Deletion of the volume in the multiple Availability Zones

B. Duplication of the volume across Regions

C. Replication of the volume in the same Availability Zone

D. Degradation of the volume across Edge locations

Answer: C

OFFICIAL EXPLANATION:

An Amazon EBS volume is a durable, block-level storage device that you can attach to a single EC2 instance. You can use EBS volumes as primary storage for data that requires frequent updates, such as the system drive for an instance or storage for a database application. You can also use them for throughput-intensive applications that perform continuous disk scans. EBS volumes persist independently from the running life of an EC2 instance.After a volume is attached to an instance, you can use it like any other physical hard drive. EBS volumes are flexible. For current-generation volumes attached to current-generation instance types, you can dynamically increase size, modify the provisioned IOPS capacity, and change volume type on live production volumes.

Read More From URL:

https://docs.aws.amazon.com/AWSEC2/latest/UserGuide/EBS Volumes.html

81. What is the type of EC2 instances you would utilize to ensure costs are minimized when you are currently hosting an infrastructure and most of the EC2 instances are nearly 90 – 100% utilized.?

A. On-Spot instances
B. Dedicated instances
C. Reserved instances
D. Full upfront reserved instances

Answer: C

OFFICIAL EXPLANATION:

When you have instances that will be used continuously and throughout the year, the best option is to buy reserved instances. By buying reserved instances, you are actually allocated an instance for the entire year or the duration you specify with a reduced cost.

Read More From URL:

https://aws.amazon.com/ec2/pricing/reserved-instances/

82. What was the first service offered by Amazon to transfer data?

A. Disk

B. Snowball

C. AWS CLI

D. AWS POLICIES

Answer: A

OFFICIAL EXPLANATION:

Disk was the first service offered by Amazon to transfer data using UPS or mail. An *instance store* provides temporary block-level storage for your instance. This storage is located on disks that are physically attached to the host computer. Instance store is ideal for temporary storage of information that changes frequently, such as buffers, caches, scratch data, and other temporary content, or for data that is replicated across a fleet of instances, such as a load-balanced pool of web servers.

Read More From URL:

https://docs.aws.amazon.com/AWSEC2/latest/UserGuide/InstanceStorage.html

83. AWS Snowball provides certain services. Which is the correct service among the given options?

A. Secure transfer to small amounts of data into and out of the AWS Cloud.

B. It's a backup solution that provides an off-premises Cloud storage.

C. Secure transfer to large amounts of data into and out of the AWS Cloud.

D. It provides an decrypted SSL startpoint for backups in the Cloud.

Answer: C

OFFICIAL EXPLANATION:

Snowball is a petabyte-scale data transport solution that uses secure appliances to transfer large amounts of data into and out of AWS. Using Snowball addresses common challenges with large-scale data transfers including high network costs, long transfer times, and security concerns. Transferring data with Snowball is simple, fast, secure, and can be as little as one-fifth the cost of high-speed Internet.

Read More From URL:

https://aws.amazon.com/snowball/

84. IT company wants to enable fast, easy, and secure transfers of files over long distances between your client and your Amazon S3 bucket. Which service provided by AWS will be most useful?

A. SNMP

B. S3 Transfer Acceleration

C. Transfer Acceleration

D. S3 Deceleration

Answer: B

OFFICIAL EXPLANATION:

Amazon S3 Transfer Acceleration enables fast, easy, and secure transfers of files over long distances between your client and an S3 bucket. Transfer Acceleration takes advantage of Amazon CloudFront's globally distributed edge locations. As the data arrives at an edge location, data is routed to Amazon S3 over an optimized network path.

Read More From URL:

http://docs.aws.amazon.com/AmazonS3/latest/dev/transfer-acceleration.html

85. Jack wanted to isolate a section of the AWS cloud, and launch AWS resources in a defined virtual network. Which of these options should he choose?

A. Virtual Private Cloud

B. Amazon RDS

C. AWS cloud9

D. Aurora

Answer: A

OFFICIAL EXPLANATION:

Amazon Virtual Private Cloud, or VPC helps you logically isolate a section of the AWS cloud, and launch AWS resources in a defined virtual network. where you can launch AWS resources in a virtual network that you define. You have complete control over your virtual networking environment, including selection of your own IP address range, creation of subnets, and configuration of route tables and network gateways. You can use both IPv4 and IPv6 in your VPC for secure and easy access to resources and applications.

You can easily customize the network configuration for your Amazon VPC. For example, you can create a public-facing subnet for your web servers that has access to the Internet, and place your backend systems such as databases or application servers in a private-facing subnet with no Internet access. You can leverage multiple layers of security, including security groups and network access control lists, to help control access to Amazon EC2 instances in each subnet.

Read More From URL:

https://aws.amazon.com/vpc/

86. Your logs show that one or more AWS-owned IP addresses are sending packets to multiple ports on your server. Also you know that, this is an attempt to discover unsecured ports. What will you do ?

A. Contact the AWS Abuse team.

B. Contact the AWS support team.

C. Contact the AWS Development team.

D. AWS security team.

Answer: A

OFFICIAL EXPLANATION:

If you suspect that AWS resources are being used for abusive purposes, contact the AWS Abuse team using the Report Amazon EC2 Abuse form, or by contacting abuse@amazonaws.com.

Provide all the necessary information, including logs in plaintext, email headers, and so on, when you submit your request.

Read More From URL:

https://aws.amazon.com/premiumsupport/knowledge-center/report-aws-abuse/

87. With the decision to store data in Amazon Glacier, the Ahana group of companies came across one of the used cases. Find the case used?

A. Back up media assets

B. Recreating Data

C. Reboot Media

D. Deleting Data

Answer: A

OFFICIAL EXPLANATION:

Amazon Glacier supports the used cases like archiving off-site enterprise information, backing up media assets, storing research and scientific data, preserving digital data, and replacing magnetic tapes. One of the core values of a data lake is that it is the collection point and repository for all of an organization's data assets, in whatever their native formats are. This enables quick ingestion, elimination of data duplication and data sprawl, and centralized governance and management. After the data assets are collected, they need to be transformed into normalized formats to be used by a variety of data analytics and processing tools.

Read More From URL:

https://docs.aws.amazon.com/aws-technical-content/latest/building-data-lakes/transforming-data-assets.html

We have taken care in preparing each question in the book., in spite of it if there are corrections to be made in the book please feel free to mail us at care@bigbangtechno.in . Our Architect will validate it and make the corresponding changes. After the changes are made, **we will publish your name with a 'Vote of Thanks' in Amazon Kindle Book Publish website.**

We hope you are satisfied with this book. **If you feel this book has helped you in some way for your preparation, please rate us 5 star in Amazon Kindle.** It will be a great moral support to us and will help us to improve the quality of the book in the forthcoming editions.

88. If you want to create snapshots from the EBS volumes in another geographical location using the console, where would you create the snapshots?

A. In same Availability Zone
B. In another Region
C. In another Corner location
D. In same region

Answer: B

OFFICIAL EXPLANATION:

With Amazon EBS, you can create point-in-time snapshots of volumes, which we store for you in Amazon S3. After you've created a snapshot and it has finished copying to Amazon S3 (when the snapshot status is completed), you can copy it from one AWS Region to another, or within the same Region. Amazon S3 server-side encryption (256-bit AES) protects a snapshot's data in-transit during a copy operation. The snapshot copy receives an ID that is different than the ID of the original snapshot.

Read More From URL:

https://docs.aws.amazon.com/AWSEC2/latest/UserGuide/ebs-copy-snapshot.html

89. The Trusted Advisor service provides insight regarding _____

A. Security, fault tolerance, high availability, and connectivity

B. Performance, cost optimization, security, and fault tolerance

C. Security and performance

D. Performance and cost optimization

Answer: B

OFFICIAL EXPLANATION:

Screenshot in below AWS Doc shows what services the Trusted Advisor Dashboard offers.

Read More From URL:

https://aws.amazon.com/premiumsupport/trustedadvisor/

90. OrangeScape Pvt. Ltd. want to transfer huge amount of public records. They needed some solution that would not charge them much. Which of the following is the most suitable ?

A. AWS Management Console

B. AWS MFA

C. CLI

D. Snowball

Answer: D

OFFICIAL EXPLANATION:

Snowball is a petabyte-scale data transport solution that uses secure appliances to transfer large amounts of data into and out of AWS. Using Snowball addresses common challenges with large-scale data transfers including high network costs, long transfer times, and security concerns. Transferring data with Snowball is simple, fast, secure, and can be as little as one-fifth the cost of high-speed Internet.

Read More From URL:

https://aws.amazon.com/snowball/

91. XYZ company wants a durable storage for static content while utilizing lower Overall CPU resources for the web tier. are deploying a 2-tier, highly available web application to AWS . At such an instance what can they prefer?

A. Amazon S3

B. Amazon EBS Snapshots

C. Amazon SES

D. Microsoft SQL

Answer: A

OFFCIAL EXPLANATION:

Amazon S3 is the default storage service that should be considered for companies. If provides durable storage for all static content.

Read More From URL:

https://aws.amazon.com/s3/

92. A company wants to use an application where there is significant amount of traffic. Which services can help them?

A. Single purpose IOPS

B. General Purpose IOPS

C. Provisioned IOPS

D. Multipurpose IOPS

Answer: C

OFFICIAL EXPLANATION:

Provisioned IOPS is used for applications and databases where there is significant amount of traffic. For production application that requires fast and consistent I/O performance, we recommend Provisioned IOPS (input/output operations per second) storage. Provisioned IOPS storage is a storage type that delivers predictable performance, and consistently low latency. Provisioned IOPS storage is optimized for online transaction processing (OLTP) workloads that have consistent performance requirements. Provisioned IOPS helps performance tuning of these workloads.

Read More From URL:

https://docs.aws.amazon.com/AmazonRDS/latest/UserGuide/CHAP_Storage.html#USER_PIOPS

93. "Principal of Least Privilege" states?

A. Users should be granted permission to access all resources

B. Users should always have more access granted to them then they need, just in case they end up needed it in the future.

C. Users should submit some access request in written so that there is no paper trail of who needs access to different AWS resources.

D. Users should be granted permission to access only resources they need to do their assigned job

Answer: D

OFFICIAL EXPLANATION:

The principle means giving a user account only those privileges which are essential to perform its intended function. For example, a user account for the sole purpose of creating backups does not need to install software: hence, it has rights only to run backup and backup-related applications.

Read More From URL:

https://en.wikipedia.org/wiki/Principle_of_least_privilege

94. Direct Attached Storage is a kind of _____ Storage.

A. Amazon Elastic Block Storage
B. Read drive
C. Hard Disk Storage
D. Internal Storage

Answer: C

OFFCIAL EXPLANATION:

Other enterprise applications like databases or ERP systems often require dedicated, low latency storage for each host. This is analogous to direct-attached storage (DAS) or a Storage Area Network (SAN). Block-based cloud storage solutions like Amazon

Elastic Block Store (EBS) are provisioned with each virtual server and offer the ultra-low latency required for high performance workloads.

Read More From URL:

https://aws.amazon.com/what-is-cloud-object-storage/

95. Your web application is generating digital policy files for verifying users. What is the best possible solution if you want to save them in a cost effective way . Once the files are verified they may not be required in the future unless there are some compliance issues.

A. AWS Glacier

B. AWS SQS

C. Aurora

D. AWS SES

Answer: A

OFFCIAL EXPLANATION:

Amazon S3 Glacier is a secure, durable, and extremely low-cost cloud storage service for data archiving and long-term backup. It is designed to deliver 99.999999999% durability, and provides comprehensive security and compliance capabilities that can help meet even the most stringent regulatory requirements. Amazon S3 Glacier provides query-in-place functionality, allowing you to run powerful analytics directly on your archive data at rest. Customers can store data for as little as $0.004 per gigabyte per month, a significant savings compared to on-premises solutions. To keep costs low yet suitable for varying retrieval needs, Amazon S3 Glacier provides three options for access to archives, from a few minutes to several hours.

Read More From URL:

https://aws.amazon.com/glacier/

96. Suppose you want to host virtual servers in the AWS Cloud , which service would you prefer?

A. AWS CLI

B. AWS Server

C. AWS Regions

D. AWS EC2

Answer: D

OFFCIAL EXPLANATION:

The AWS Documentation mentions the following Amazon Elastic Compute Cloud (Amazon EC2) is a web service that provides secure, resizable compute capacity in the cloud. It is designed to make web-scale cloud computing easier for developers.

Read More From URL:

https://aws.amazon.com/ec2/

97. _____ means that the storage is temporary, and its contents can be lost when the system is rebooted.

A. Peripheral

B. Single Purpose IOPS

C. Ephemeral

D. Multi Purpose IOPS

Answer: C

OFFCIAL EXPLANATION:

Depending on the EC2 instance type selected, there will also be from zero to 24 instance-store volumes automatically available to the instance. Instance-store volumes provide temporary block-level storage to the instance. The data in an instance store persists only during the lifetime of its associated instance. Because of the temporary nature of instance-store volumes, they are often referred to as ""ephemeral""—not lasting, enduring, or permanent".

.

Read More From URL:

https://aws.amazon.com/blogs/developer/stripe-windows-ephemeral-disks-at-launch/

98. What are the norms specified by cloud architecture principle of elasticity:

A. Create systems that scale to the required capacity based on changes on demand

B. Decelerate the design process because recovery from failure is manual

C. Create systems that do not scale to the required capacity based on changes on demand .

D. Maximize storage requirements by reducing logging and auditing activities

Answer: A

OFFCIAL EXPLANATION:

Elasticity allows you to match the supply of resources—which cost money—to demand. Because cloud resources are paid for based on usage, matching needs to utilization is critical for cost optimization. Demand includes both external usage, such as the number of customers who visit a website over a given period, and internal usage, such as an application team using development and test environments.

Read More From URL:

https://docs.aws.amazon.com/aws-technical-content/latest/cost-optimization-automating-elasticity/cost-optimization-automating-elasticity.pdf

99. EC2 Instances hosted in AWS must be protected using which of the below options? Choose 2

A. Usage of MOPS
B. Usage of Security Groups
C. Usage of Network Access Control Lists
D. Usage of the MFA

Answer: B, C.

OFFICIAL EXPLANATION:

The AWS Documentation mentions the following A security group acts as a virtual firewall for your instance to control inbound and outbound traffic. A network access control list (ACL) is an optional layer of security for your VPC. that acts as a firewall for controlling traffic in and out of one or more subnets.

Read More From URL:

https://docs.aws.amazon.com/AmazonVPC/latest/UserGuide/V PC_SecurityGroups.html.

https://docs.aws.amazon.com/AmazonVPC/latest/UserGuide/V PC_ACLs.html

100. For transfer of a website to one type of cloud while its brochure is on another, which cloud can be used?

A. Real Cloud

B. Private Cloud

C. Dynamic Cloud

D. Hybrid Cloud

Answer: D

OFFCIAL EXPLANATION:

Through hybrid cloud, a company is able to retain control over an internally managed private cloud, while depending on the public cloud, when required. For example, during peak time, you can migrate a few applications to the public cloud. In cloud computing, hybrid cloud refers to the use of both on-premises resources in addition to public cloud resources. A hybrid cloud enables an organization to migrate applications and data to the cloud, extend their datacenter capacity, utilize new cloud-native capabilities, move applications closer to customers, and create a backup and disaster recovery solution with cost-effective high availability.

Read More From URL:

https://aws.amazon.com/enterprise/hybrid/

101.Your company is planning on using the AWS EC2 service to create golden images of their deployed Operating system. Which of the following correspond to a golden image in AWS.

A. Amazon Machines Images

B. EBS Snapshots

C. Amazon S3

D. Amazon CloudWatch

Answer: A

OFFICIAL EXPLANATION:

The AWS Documentation mentions the following An Amazon Machine Image (AMI) provides the information required to launch an instance, which is a virtual server in the cloud. You specify an AMI when you launch an instance, and you can launch as many instances from the AMI as you need. You can also launch instances from as many different AMIs as you need.

Read More From URL:

https://docs.aws.amazon.com/AWSEC2/latest/UserGuide/AMIs
.html

102. CloudFormation Components Templates has a format that conforms to the ____.

A. HTTP

B. HTML

C. JavaScript Object Notation

D. STP

Answer: B

OFFICIAL EXPLANATION:

Read More From URL:

103. A company wants to ensure low-latency delivery. How does Amazon CloudFront help?

A. AWS multiple locations

B. AWS Corner locations

C. Amazon Virtual Private Cloud (Amazon VPC)

D. AWS edge locations

Answer: D

OFFICIAL EXPLANATION:

The AWS global infrastructure delivers a cloud infrastructure companies can depend on—no matter their size, changing needs, or challenges. The AWS Global Infrastructure is designed and built to deliver the most flexible, reliable, scalable, and secure cloud computing environment with the highest quality global network performance available today. Every component of the AWS infrastructure is design and built for redundancy and reliability, from regions to networking links to load balancers to routers and firmware using AWS Edge locations

Read More From URL:

https://aws.amazon.com/about-aws/global-infrastructure/

104. Which of the below steps would you carry out to ensure the PCI compliance of AWS is met for the application. Choose 2 answers from the following.

A. Choose AWS services which are PCI Compliant

B. Audit before the deployment of the application for PCI Compliance

C. Ensure the AWS Services are made PCI Compliant

D. Ensure the right steps are taken during application development for PCI Compliance

Answer: A, D

OFFICIAL EXPLANATION:

The snapshot from the AWS Documentation mentions that some of the AWS services are already PCI compliant. This list should be checked when designing the application.

Read More From URL:

https://aws.amazon.com/compliance/pci-dss-level-1-faqs/

105. Stack as single unit refers to?

A. Blueprint for creating and configuring resources

B. CloudFormation service rolls back the stack or deletes

C. Develop highly scalable, reliable, and lucrative applications

D. Deploys the independent resources

Answer: B

OFFICIAL EXPLANATION:

AWS CloudFormation service rolls back the stack or deletes any created resources if even one resource fails to successfully create itself. A stack is a collection of AWS resources that you can manage as a single unit. In other words, you can create, update, or delete a collection of resources by creating, updating, or deleting stacks. All the resources in a stack are defined by the stack's AWS CloudFormation template. A stack, for instance, can include all the resources required to run a web application, such as a web server, a database, and networking rules. If you no longer require that web application, you can simply delete the stack, and all of its related resources are deleted.

Read More From URL:

https://docs.aws.amazon.com/AWSCloudFormation/latest/User Guide/stacks.html

106.What is the advantage of decoupling an application?

A. Create a loosely integrated application

B. Enable data synchronization across the web application layer.

C. Reduce inter-dependencies so failures do not impact other components

D. Increase inter-dependencies so failures do not impact other components

Answer: C

OFFICIAL EXPLANATION:

AWS Server Migration Service (SMS) now offers multi-server migration support that makes it easier and more cost effective to migrate applications from on-premises datacenters to Amazon EC2. You can migrate a group of servers as a single unit without having to go through the hassle of coordinating the replication of individual servers or decoupling application dependencies. With multi-server support, Server Migration Service significantly reduces the time to migrate applications and lessens the risk of errors in the migration process.

Read More From URL:

https://aws.amazon.com/about-aws/whats-new/2018/12/aws-server-migration-service-adds-support-for-multi-server-migration/

107.Which can be used to get data onto Amazon Glacier? Choose 3 answers from the options given below.

A. AWS Glacier API

B. AWS Glacier SDK

C. AWS EC2 Dashboard

D. AWS S3 Lifecycle policies

Answer: A, B, D

OFFICIAL EXPLANATION:

Note that the AWS Console cannot be used to upload data onto Glacier. The console can only be used to create a Glacier vault which can be used to upload the data. Amazon S3 Glacier (Glacier) provides a management console, which you can use to create and delete vaults. However, you cannot upload archives to Glacier by using the management console. To upload data, such as photos, videos, and other documents, you must either use the AWS CLI or write code to make requests, by using either the REST API directly or by using the AWS SDKs.

Read More From URL:

https://docs.aws.amazon.com/amazonglacier/latest/dev/uploading-an-archive.html

108. Suppose you want to access the provided service in AWS, what do you prefer?

A. AWS Security Groups

B. AWS Hardware Development Kits

C. AWS Software Development Kits

D. AWS Enquiry API?s

Answer: C

OFFICIAL EXPLANATION

User can access Amazon Web Services through Management Console, Command Line Interface, Command Line Tools, AWS Software Development Kits, and Query APIs.

Read More From URL:

https://aws.amazon.com/tools/

109. Prozone company wants to carve out a portion of the AWS Cloud , in such a case which service do you prefer for them?

A. AWS VPC

B. AWS edge locations

C. AWS Subnets

D. AWS Regions

Answer: A

OFFICIAL EXPLANATION:

Amazon Virtual Private Cloud, or VPC helps you logically isolate a section of the AWS cloud, and launch AWS resources in a defined virtual network. where you can launch AWS resources in a virtual network that you define. You have complete control over your virtual networking environment, including selection of your own IP address range, creation of subnets, and configuration of route tables and network gateways. You can use both IPv4 and IPv6 in your VPC for secure and easy access to resources and applications.

You can easily customize the network configuration for your Amazon VPC. For example, you can create a public-facing subnet for your web servers that has access to the Internet, and place your backend systems such as databases or application servers in a private-facing subnet with no Internet access. You can leverage multiple layers of security, including security groups and network access control lists, to help control access to Amazon EC2 instances in each subnet.

Read More From URL:

https://aws.amazon.com/vpc/

110. Choose the AWS Support plan that gives access to a Support Concierge :

A. Basic

B. Business

C. On demand

D. Enterprise

Answer: D

OFFICIAL EXPLANATION

AWS Enterprise Support provides you with concierge-like service where the main focus is helping you achieve your outcomes and find success in the cloud.

Read More From URL:

https://aws.amazon.com/premiumsupport/plans/enterprise/

https://aws.amazon.com/premiumsupport/compare-plans/

111. If you can mention the values of the parameters at the time of creating the stack, and you can specify input parameters, it means you are _____.

A. Inserting Stack

B. Create Stack

C. Reusing Template

D. Deleting Template

Answer: B

OFFICIAL EXPLANATION:

Creates a stack as specified in the template. After the call completes successfully, the stack creation starts. A list of `Parameter` structures that specify input parameters for the stack. For more information, see the Parameter data type.

Read More From URL:

https://docs.aws.amazon.com/cli/latest/reference/cloudformatio n/create-stack.html

112. Derek noticed that he is paying for way more server capacity than is required. What AWS feature should Derek set up and configure to ensure that his application is automatically adding/removing server capacity to keep in line with the required demand?

A. AWS EBS

B. AWS Trusted Advisor

C. AWS EC2

D. AWS Autoscaling

Answer: D

OFFICIAL EXPLANATION:

AWS Auto Scaling monitors your applications and automatically adjusts capacity to maintain steady, predictable performance at the lowest possible cost. Using AWS Auto Scaling, it's easy to setup application scaling for multiple resources across multiple services in minutes. The service provides a simple, powerful user interface that lets you build scaling plans for resources including Amazon EC2 instances and Spot Fleets, Amazon ECStasks, Amazon DynamoDB tables and indexes, and Amazon Aurora Replicas. AWS Auto Scaling makes scaling simple with recommendations that allow you to optimize performance, costs, or balance between them. If you're already using Amazon EC2 Auto Scaling to dynamically scale your Amazon EC2 instances, you can now combine it with AWS Auto Scaling to scale additional resources for other AWS services. With AWS Auto Scaling, your applications always have the right resources at the right time.

Read More From URL:

https://aws.amazon.com/autoscaling/

113. A company is planning to use AWS and most of their systems

are business critical and need to have response times less than 15 minutes. Which of the following support plans can they make use of?

A. Basic

B. Reserved

C. Enterprise

D. Spot

Answer: C

OFFICIAL EXPLANATION

Only the Enterprise support plan fits this requirement.

Read More From URL:

https://aws.amazon.com/premiumsupport/compare-plans/

114. What services should a company use to monitor cloud resources such as Amazon EC2 and Amazon RDS instances, and applications.

A. Amazon Glacier

B. Amazon CloudWatch

C. Amazon S3

D. Amazon EBS

Answer: B

OFFICIAL EXPLANATION:

Amazon CloudWatch refers to a service that allows real-time monitoring of your cloud resources such as, Amazon EC2 and Amazon RDS instances, and applications. Amazon CloudWatch is a monitoring and management service built for developers, system operators, site reliability engineers (SRE), and IT managers. CloudWatch provides you with data and actionable insights to monitor your applications, understand and respond to system-wide performance changes, optimize resource utilization, and get a unified view of operational health. CloudWatch collects monitoring and operational data in the form of logs, metrics, and events, providing you with a unified view of AWS resources, applications and services that run on AWS, and on-premises servers. You can use CloudWatch to set high resolution alarms, visualize logs and metrics side by side, take automated actions, troubleshoot issues, and discover insights to optimize your applications, and ensure they are running smoothly.

Read More From URL:

https://aws.amazon.com/cloudwatch/

115. A company planning to introduce a new product is expecting a high traffic to their web application. As part of Enterprise support plan, which of the following could provide them with an architectural and scaling guidance?

A. AWS Cloud9

B. AWS Console

C. Amazon Redshift

D. Infrastructure Event Management Service

Answer: D:

OFFICIAL EXPLANATION:

AWS Enterprise Support provides you with concierge-like service where the main focus is helping you achieve your outcomes and find success in the cloud.

With Enterprise Support, you get 24x7 technical support from high-quality engineers, tools and technology to automatically manage health of your environment, consultative architectural guidance delivered in the context of your applications and use-cases, and a designated Technical Account Manager (TAM) to coordinate access to proactive / preventative programs and AWS subject matter experts.

Read More From URL:

https://aws.amazon.com/premiumsupport/plans/enterprise/

116. Which of the following is NOT a feature of an edge location:

A. Distribute load across multiple resources

B. Cache multiple responses

C. Distribute load across one resource

D. Used in conjunction with the Cloudfront service

Answer: A

OFFICIAL EXPLANATION:

The Edge location does not do the job of distributing load. It is used in conjunction with the Cloudfront service to cache the objects and deliver content.

Read More From URL:

https://aws.amazon.com/cloudfront/details/

117. How can Amazon CloudWatch be used?

A. Amazon Glacier

B. Amazon Route 53

C. Amazon Virtual Private Cloud

D. AWS Free Tier

Answer : D

OFFICIAL EXPLANATION:

You can get started with Amazon CloudWatch for free. Most AWS Services (EC2, S3, Kinesis, etc.) vend metrics automatically for free to CloudWatch. Many applications should be able to operate within these free tier limits. You can learn more about AWS Free Tier here.

.

Read More From URL:

https://aws.amazon.com/cloudwatch/pricing/

118. PBC Pvt Ltd, an infotech company wants to manage services through a web-based user interface. Which service will makes them to enable this?

A. AWS Application Programming Interface (API)

B. AWS HDK(Hardware Development Kits)

C. AWS Software Development Kit (SDK)

D. AWS Management Console

Answer: D

OFFICIAL EXPLANATION:

The AWS Management console allows you to access and manage Amazon Web Services through a simple and intuitive web-based user interface. The AWS Management Console is a web application that comprises and refers to a broad collection of service consoles for managing Amazon Web Services. When you first sign in, you see the console home page. The home page provides access to each service console as well as an intuitive user interface for exploring AWS and getting helpful tips. Among other things, the individual service consoles offer tools for working with Amazon S3 buckets, launching and connecting to Amazon EC2 instances, setting Amazon CloudWatch alarms, and getting information about your account and about billing

Read More From URL:

https://aws.amazon.com/console/

119. The stored objects should be enabled such that it can be downloaded via a URL. Which storage option would you choose?

A. Amazon Storage Gateway

B. Amazon Glacier

C. Amazon S3

D. Amazon Cloud9

Answer: C

OFFICIAL EXPLANATION:

Amazon S3 is the perfect storage option. It also provides the facility of assigning a URL to each object which can be used to download the object.

Read More From URL:

https://aws.amazon.com/s3/

120. When public and private cloud services are mixed , the cloud formed will be?

A. Private Cloud

B. Public Cloud

C. Real Cloud

D. Hybrid Cloud

Answer: D

OFFCIAL EXPLANATION:

Through hybrid cloud, a company is able to retain control over an internally managed private cloud, while depending on the public cloud, when required. For example, during peak time, you can migrate a few applications to the public cloud. In cloud computing, hybrid cloud refers to the use of both on-premises resources in addition to public cloud resources. A hybrid cloud enables an organization to migrate applications and data to the cloud, extend their datacenter capacity, utilize new cloud-native capabilities, move applications closer to customers, and create a backup and disaster recovery solution with cost-effective high availability.

Read More From URL:

https://aws.amazon.com/enterprise/hybrid/

121. What is meant by "Principal of Least Privilege"?

A. Users should be granted permission to access only resources they need to do their assigned job

B. Users should be granted permission to access all resources they need to do their assigned job

C. Users should submit all access request in written so that there is a paper trail of who needs access to different AWS resources.

D. All users should have different baseline permissions granted to them to use basic AWS services.

Answer: A

OFFICIAL EXPLANATION:

a IAM policy that uses the principal of least privilege to grant access rights, and associated that policy with a role.

Read More From URL:

https://docs.aws.amazon.com/pinpoint/latest/developerguide/tut

orials-two-way-sms-next-steps.html

122. To host a database server for a minimum period of one year, which of the following would result in the least cost?

A. Spot Instances

B. . Partial Upfront costs Reserved

C. No Upfront costs Reserved

D. On demand Instances

Answer: B

OFFICIAL EXPLANATION:

If the database is going to be used for a minimum of one year at least , then it is better to get Reserved Instances. You can save on costs , and if you use a partial upfront options , you can get a better discount

Read More From URL:

https://aws.amazon.com/ec2/pricing/reserved-instances/

123. What are the benefits of Amazon Web Services in Amazon's cloud computing environment?

A. Economies of scale

B. 1000 petabytes of free service

C. 50 gigabytes free service

D. Lifetime free Service

Answer: C

OFFICIAL EXPLANATION:

Refer the URL

Read More From URL:

https://aws.amazon.com/free/faqs/

126. Which of the following services would help you analyze performance issues in an under developed application using microservices architecture?

A. AWS X-Ray

B. AWS Code Pipeline

C. AWS Security groups

D. AWS Management console

Answer: A

OFFICIAL EXPLANATION:

AWS X-Ray helps developers analyze and debug production, distributed applications, such as those built using a microservices architecture. With X-Ray, you can understand how your application and its underlying services are performing to identify and troubleshoot the root cause of performance issues and errors. X-Ray provides an end-to-end view of requests as they travel through your application, and shows a map of your application's underlying components. You can use X-Ray to analyze both applications in development and in production, from simple three-tier applications to complex microservices applications consisting of thousands of services

Read More From URL:

https://aws.amazon.com/xray/

127. In a company using AWS there is a requirement for a development and test environment for 3 months. Which would they prefer to use?

A. Spot Instances

B. Basic Instances

C. Upfront costs Reserved

D. On-Demand

Answer: D

OFFICIAL EXPLANATION:

Since the requirement is just for 3 months, then the best cost effective option is to use On-Demand Instances.

Read More From URL:

https://aws.amazon.com/ec2/pricing/on-demand/

128. Magnetic storage is a persistent type of slower, older _____.

A. Amazon Glazier

B. Short term Storage

C. Amazon S3

113

D. Elastic File System

Answer: A

Amazon S3 Glacier is a secure, durable, and extremely low-cost cloud storage service for data archiving and long-term backup. It is designed to deliver 99.999999999% durability, and provides comprehensive security and compliance capabilities that can help meet even the most stringent regulatory requirements. Amazon S3 Glacier provides query-in-place functionality, allowing you to run powerful analytics directly on your archive data at rest. Customers can store data for as little as $0.004 per gigabyte per month, a significant savings compared to on-premises solutions. To keep costs low yet suitable for varying retrieval needs, Amazon S3 Glacier provides three options for access to archives, from a few minutes to several hours.

Read More From URL:

https://aws.amazon.com/glacier/

129. Which can be a good use case for storing content in AWS RRS?

A. Storing large video files.
B. Storing thumbnails & transcoded media
C. Storing a video file which is not producible
D. Storing frequently used log files.

Answer: B

OFFICIAL EXPLANATION:

Storing thumbnails & transcoded media is one of the good use case for storing content in AWS RRS which can be used for later use.

Read More From URL:

https://docs.aws.amazon.com/AWSRRS/latest/Storingcontent.ht ml

130. When creating security groups, which of the following is a responsibility of the customer. Choose 2 answers:

A. Giving a name and description for all the security group

B . Ensure the rules are applied After a period of time

C. Defining the rules as per the customer requirements.

D. Ensure the security groups are linked to the Elastic Network interface

Answer: A, C

OFFICIAL EXPLANATION:

When you define security rules for EC2 Instances, you give a name, description and write the rules for the security group.

Read More From URL:

https://docs.aws.amazon.com/AWSEC2/latest/UserGuide/using -network-security.html

131. Virtual Tape Library provides users with an unlimited _____.

A. Collection of real tapes

B. Collection of Cassette library

C. Physical Space

D. Collection of virtual tapes

Answer: D

OFFICIAL EXPLANATION:

Virtual Tape Library provides users with an unlimited collection of virtual tapes. It provides and lets the user control an existing tape-based backup application n, Gateway-Virtual Tape Library (Gateway-VTL). Gateway-VTL is the newest addition to AWS Storage Gateway, a service that integrates your on-premises IT environment with AWS storage. With Gateway-VTL, AWS Storage Gateway now provides you with a cost-effective, scalable, and durable virtual tape infrastructure that allows you to eliminate the challenges associated with owning and operating an on-premises physical tape infrastructure.

With Gateway-VTL you can have a limitless collection of virtual tapes. Each virtual tape can be stored in a Virtual Tape Library backed by Amazon S3 or a Virtual Tape Shelf backed by Amazon Glacier. The Virtual Tape Library exposes an industry standard iSCSI interface which provides your backup application with on-line access to the virtual tapes. When you no longer require immediate or frequent access to data contained on a virtual tape, you can use your backup application to move it from its Virtual Tape Library to your Virtual Tape Shelf in order to further reduce your storage costs.

Read More From URL:

https://aws.amazon.com/about-aws/whats-new/2013/11/05/aws-storage-gateway-announces-gateway-virtual-tape-library/

132. Which AWS services helps you to determine "Who terminated the Amazon EC2 Instances"?

A. AWS CloudTrail

B. Amazon EC2 instance usage report

C. Amazon CloudWatch

D. AWS Cloud9

Answer: A

OFFICIAL EXPLANATION:

AWS CloudTrail is a service that enables governance, compliance, operational auditing, and risk auditing of your AWS account. With CloudTrail, you can log, continuously monitor, and retain account activity related to actions across your AWS infrastructure. CloudTrail provides event history of your AWS account activity, including actions taken through the AWS Management Console, AWS SDKs, command line tools, and other AWS services. This event history simplifies security analysis, resource change tracking, and troubleshooting.

Read More From URL:

https://aws.amazon.com/cloudtrail/

133. What are the advantages of having infrastructure hosted on the AWS Cloud? Choose 2 answers:

A. Having the pay as you go model

B. Having complete control over the physical infrastructure

C. zero Upfront costs

D. No need to worry about security

Answer: A, C

OFFICIAL EXPLANATION:

The Physical infrastructure is a responsibility of AWS and not with the customer. Hence it is not an advantage of moving to the AWS Cloud And AWS provides security mechanisms, but even the responsibility of security lies with the customer.

Read More From URL:

https://docs.aws.amazon.com/aws-technical-content/latest/aws-overview/six-advantages-of-cloud-computing.html

134. What are the current list of service groups in the All AWS Services section?

A Networking

B Mirroring

C Data Analytics

D Redirecting

Answer: B

OFFICIAL EXPLANATION:

Amazon RDS supports Multi-AZ deployments for Microsoft SQL Server by using either SQL Server Database Mirroring (DBM) or

Always On Availability Groups (AGs). Amazon RDS monitors and maintains the health of your Multi-AZ deployment. If problems occur, RDS automatically repairs unhealthy DB instances, reestablishes synchronization, and initiates failovers. Failover only occurs if the standby and primary are fully in sync. You don't have to manage anything.

Read More From URL:

https://docs.aws.amazon.com/AmazonRDS/latest/UserGuide/USER_SQLServerMultiAZ.html

135. When choosing the instance type of services like Amazon RDS, Amazon Redshift, and Amazon Elasticsearch , which of the following is a main factor to consider with the reduction in cost?

A. Your team experience with these services.

B. Workload utilization of CPU & RAM.

C. The type of your current off-premise database.

D. Workload utilization of RAM.

Answer: B

OFFICIAL EXPLANATION:

After you have defined your monitoring goals and have created your monitoring plan, the next step is to establish a baseline for normal Amazon EC2 performance in your environment. You should measure Amazon EC2 performance at various times and under different load conditions. As you monitor Amazon EC2, you should store a history of monitoring data that you've collected. You can compare current Amazon EC2 performance to this historical data to help you to identify normal performance patterns and performance anomalies, and devise methods to address them. For example, you can monitor CPU utilization, disk I/O, and network utilization for your EC2 instances. When performance falls outside your established baseline, you might need to reconfigure or optimize the instance to reduce CPU utilization, improve disk I/O, or reduce network traffic.

Read More From URL:

https://docs.aws.amazon.com/AWSEC2/latest/UserGuide/monit oring_ec2.html

136. The IT auditor of your company needs to have a log of all access to the AWS resources in the company's account. Which of the below services can assist in providing these details?

A. AWS CloudTrail

B. AWS Groups

C. AWS EC2

D. AWS CloudFront

Answer: A

OFFICIAL EXPLANATION:

Using CloudTrail , one can monitor all the API activity conducted on all AWS services. The AWS Documentation additionally mentions the following AWS CloudTrail is a service that enables governance, compliance, operational auditing, and risk auditing of your AWS account. With CloudTrail, you can log, continuously monitor, and retain account activity related to actions across your AWS infrastructure. CloudTrail provides event history of your AWS account activity, including actions taken through the AWS Management Console, AWS SDKs, command line tools, and other AWS services. This event history simplifies security analysis, resource change tracking, and troubleshooting.

Read More From URL:

https://aws.amazon.com/cloudtrail/

137. Choose any one singular feature of AWS?

A. Resilient product structure

B. Resilient departmental structure

C. Resilient industrial structure

D. Resilient organizational structure

Answer: D

OFFICIAL EXPLANATION:

A striking feature of AWS is its resilient organizational structure. AWS has developed the Well-Architected Framework to help customers architect their mission-critical applications on AWS with secure, high-performing, resilient, and efficient infrastructure. Well Architected can help you build and deploy faster, lower or mitigate risks, make informed decisions, and learn AWS best practices.

Read More From URL:

https://aws.amazon.com/government-education/

138. A company is keen that the data on EBS volumes is safe always. What should they do?

A. Create EBS snapshots

B. Delete the data when the device is destroyed

C. Delete EBS snapshots

D. Create copies of EBS Volumes

Answer : A

OFFICIAL EXPLANATION:

A point-in-time snapshot of an EBS volume, can be used as a baseline for new volumes or for data backup. If you make periodic snapshots of a volume, the snapshots are incremental—only the blocks on the device that have changed after your last snapshot are saved in the new snapshot. Even though snapshots are saved incrementally, the snapshot deletion process is designed so that you need to retain only the most recent snapshot in order to restore the entire volume.

Read More From URL:

https://docs.aws.amazon.com/AWSEC2/latest/UserGuide/ebs-creating-snapshot.html

139. For data redundancy across regions, which feature of RDS can be used?

A. Direct region replication

B. Deleting snapshots

C. Creating Read Replica's

D. Using Multi-AZ feature

Answer: C

OFFICIAL EXPLANATION:

One can use the Read Replica feature of the database to ensure the data is replicated to another region. Amazon RDS provides high availability and failover support for DB instances using Multi-AZ deployments. Amazon RDS uses several different technologies to provide failover support. Multi-AZ deployments for Oracle, PostgreSQL, MySQL, and MariaDB DB instances use Amazon's failover technology. SQL Server DB instances use SQL Server Database Mirroring (DBM).

Read More From URL:

https://aws.amazon.com/blogs/aws/cross-region-read-replicas-for-amazon-rds-for-mysql/

140. The least privileged criteria grants _____ ?

A. Authorized access

B. Private access

C. denied public access

D. General access

Answer: A

OFFICIAL EXPLANATION:

Only authorized access is granted as per the least privileged criteria.

141. Which AWS services will help to make a scalable software with the AWS infrastructure in a scenario where a user has created photo editing software and hosted it on EC2. The software accepts requests from the user about the photo format and resolution and sends a message to S3 to enhance the picture accordingly.

A. AWS Simple Notification Service

B. AWS SES

C. AWS Simple Queue Service

D. Aurora

Answer: C

OFFICIAL EXPLANATION:

Amazon Simple Queue Service (SQS) is a fully managed message queuing service that enables you to decouple and scale microservices, distributed systems, and serverless applications. SQS eliminates the complexity and overhead associated with managing and operating message oriented middleware, and empowers developers to focus on differentiating work. Using SQS, you can send, store, and receive messages between software components at any volume, without losing messages or requiring other services to be available. Get started with SQS in minutes using the AWS console, Command Line Interface or SDK of your choice, and three simple commands.

Read More From URL:

https://aws.amazon.com/sqs/

142. Your company has a requirement to create snapshots from the EBS volumes attached to the EC2 Instances in another geographical location. Where should the company create the snapshots?

A. In another Availability Zone
B. In another region
C. In same Region
D. In same availability zone

Answer: B

OFFICIAL EXPLANATION:

Regions correspond to different geographic locations in AWS.

Read More From URL:

https://docs.aws.amazon.com/AmazonRDS/latest/UserGuide/Concepts.RegionsAndAvailabilityZones.html

143. Select one of the vital feature on Navigation Bar?

A. AWS S3
B. AWS Monitor Control

C. AWS Menu bar

D. AWS Region

Answer: D

OFFICIAL EXPLANATION:

AWS Region is another vital feature on the Navigation Bar. If a service supports Regions, the resources in each Region are independent. For example, if you create an Amazon EC2 instance or an Amazon SQS queue in one Region, the instance or queue is independent from instances or queues in another Region.

Read More From URL:

https://docs.aws.amazon.com/general/latest/gr/rande.html

144. What does Amazon ElastiCache provide?

A. A managed In-memory cache service.

B. A virtual server with a Small amount of memory.

C. A managed Out-memory cache service

D. An Amazon EC2 instance with the Memcached software already pre-installed.

Answer: A

OFFICIAL EXPLANATION:

Amazon ElastiCache offers fully managed Redis and Memcached. Seamlessly deploy, run, and scale popular open source compatible in-memory data stores. Build data-intensive apps or improve the performance of your existing apps by retrieving data from high throughput and low latency in-memory data stores. Amazon ElastiCache is a popular choice for Gaming, Ad-Tech, Financial Services, Healthcare, and IoT apps.

Read More From URL:

https://aws.amazon.com/elasticache/

145. How would you ideally implement a self-managed database in AWS.?

A. Using the AWS DynamoDB service

B. Hosting a database on an EC2 Instance

C. Hosting a database on an Amazon RDS service

D. Hosting a database on an Amazon EBS service

Answer: B

OFFICIAL EXPLANATION:

If you want a self-managed database, that means you want complete control over the database engine and the underlying infrastructure. In such a case you need to host the database on an EC2 Instance.

Read More From URL:

https://aws.amazon.com/ec2/

146. "Amazon DynamoDB" in Amazon Web Services refers to a service that offers _____.

A. SQL database

B. Solid State Disks

C. AURORA Database Models

D. NoSQL databases

Answer: B

OFFICIAL EXPLANATION:

Amazon DynamoDB is a solid state disk key-value and document database that delivers single-digit millisecond performance at any scale. It's a fully managed, multiregion, multimaster database with built-in security, backup and restore, and in-memory caching for internet-scale applications. DynamoDB can handle more than 10 trillion requests per day and support peaks of more than 20 million requests per second.

Read More From URL:

https://aws.amazon.com/dynamodb/

147. What is the payment model you are going to use when you decide to pay a low upfront fee and get a significantly discounted hourly rate.?

A. Pay even less when AWS degrades

B. Pay more when you reserve

C. Pay even less as AWS grows

D. Pay less when you reserve

Answer: D

OFFICIAL EXPLANATION:

Reserved Instances with a higher upfront payment provide greater discounts. You can also find Reserved Instances offered by third-party sellers at lower prices and shorter terms on theReserved Instance Marketplace.

Read More From URL:

https://aws.amazon.com/ec2/pricing/reserved-instances/

148. Which of the following is a compatible MySQL database which also has the ability to grow in storage size on its own.

A. RDS Microsoft NoSQL Server
B. GLACIER
C. Aurora
D. RDS MySQL

Answer: C

OFFICIAL EXPLANATION:

The AWS Documentation mentions the following Amazon Aurora (Aurora) is a fully managed, MySQL- and PostgreSQL-compatible, relational database engine. It combines the speed and reliability of high-end commercial databases with the simplicity and cost-effectiveness of open-source databases. It delivers up to five times the throughput of MySQL and up to three times the throughput of PostgreSQL without requiring changes to most of your existing applications.

Read More From URL:

https://docs.aws.amazon.com/AmazonRDS/latest/UserGuide/Aurora.Overview.html

149. Can you suggest any other name for attributes?

A. Series
B. Indexes
C. Fields
D. Keys

Answer: C

OFFICIAL EXPLANATION:

The attributes are also called columns or fields.

150. Medimax Company needs to automate the creation of sandbox accounts for developers and grant entities in those accounts access only to the necessary AWS services. Which of the following would help?

A. AWS Trusted Advisor

B. Amazon Dev Pay

C. Amazon VMware

D. AWS organizations

Answer: D

OFFICIAL EXPLANATION:

WS Organizations helps you centrally govern your environment as you grow and scale your workloads on AWS. Whether you are a growing startup or a large enterprise, Organizations helps you to centrally manage billing; control access, compliance, and security; and share resources across your AWS accounts.Using AWS Organizations, you can automate account creation, create groups of accounts to reflect your business needs, and apply policies for these groups for governance. You can also simplify billing by setting up a single payment method for all of your AWS accounts. Through integrations with other AWS services, you can use Organizations to define central configurations and resource sharing across accounts in your organization. AWS Organizations is available to all AWS customers at no additional charge.

Read More From URL:

https://aws.amazon.com/organizations/

151.Which of the following statements are TRUE about elasticity.
Choose 2 answers:

A. Diverting traffic to instances with higher capacity

B. Diverting traffic to instances with the least load

C. Diverting traffic across Same regions

D. Diverting traffic to instances based on the demand

Answer: B,D

OFFICIAL EXPLANATION:
The concept of Elasticity is the means of an application having the ability to scale up and scale down based on demand. An example of such a service is the Autoscaling service.

Read More From URL:
https://aws.amazon.com/autoscaling/

152. Select the Dynamo data types which includes a string set, a binary set, and a number set?

A. vector

B. Development

C. Set

D. None of the above

Answer: C

OFFICIAL EXPLANATION:
Amazon DynamoDB supports three major categories of data types. Set is a data types that includes a string set, a binary set, and a number set.

Read More From URL:
https://docs.aws.amazon.com/amazondynamodb/latest/develope rguide/HowItWorks.NamingRulesDataTypes.html

153. Your company wants fast, easy, and secure transfers of files over long distances between your client and your Amazon S3 bucket, at such an instance what will you choose?

A. Snowball

B. FTP Snowball Transfer

C. AWS Aurora

D. S3 Transfer Acceleration

Answer: D

OFFICIAL EXPLANATION:

Amazon S3 Transfer Acceleration enables fast, easy, and secure transfers of files over long distances between your client and an S3 bucket. Transfer Acceleration takes advantage of Amazon CloudFront's globally distributed edge locations. As the data arrives at an edge location, data is routed to Amazon S3 over an optimized network path.

Read More From URL:

https://docs.aws.amazon.com/AmazonS3/latest/dev/transfer-acceleration.html

154. How does Elastic load balancer work?

A. To distribute traffic to AWS resources across multiple regions

B. To distribute traffic to one EC2 Instances

C. To distribute traffic to multiple EC2 Instances

D. To Decrease the size of the EC2 Instance based on demand

Answer: C

OFFICIAL EXPLANATION:

The AWS Documentation mentions the following A load balancer distributes incoming application traffic across multiple EC2 instances in multiple Availability Zones. This increases the fault tolerance of your applications. Elastic Load Balancing detects unhealthy instances and routes traffic only to healthy instances.

Read More From URL:

https://docs.aws.amazon.com/elasticloadbalancing/latest/classic/introduction.html

155. Which of the following has a unique decimal number or a code point?

A. Unicode character

B. Primary Code Character

C. Decimal Code Character

D. Binary code Character

Answer: A

OFFICIAL EXPLANATION:

Each Unicode character has a unique decimal number or a code point.

Read More From URL:

https://docs.aws.amazon.com/AmazonRDS/latest/UserGuide/Appendix.SQLServer.CommonDBATasks.Collation.html

156. A company currently uses VM Templates to spin up virtual machines on their on-premise infrastructure. Which of the following can be used to spin up EC2 instances on the AWS Cloud?

A. Amazon SDK

B. Amazon VMware

C. EBS Snapshots

D. Amazon Machines Images

Answer: D

OFFICIAL EXPLANATION:

An Amazon Machine Image (AMI) provides the information required to launch an instance. You must specify an AMI when you launch an instance. You can launch multiple instances from a single AMI when you need multiple instances with the same configuration. You can use different AMIs to launch instances when you need instances with different configurations.

Read More From URL:

https://docs.aws.amazon.com/AWSEC2/latest/UserGuide/AMIs.html

157. Which of the following is the concept of Autoscaling ?

A. To scale down resources based on demand

B. To distribute traffic to multiple EC2 Instances

C. To distribute traffic to AWS resources across multiple regions

D. To scale up resources based on demand

Answer: D

OFFICIAL EXPLANATION:

The AWS Documentation mentions the following AWS Auto Scaling monitors your applications and automatically adjusts capacity to maintain steady, predictable performance at the lowest possible cost. Using AWS Auto Scaling, it's easy to setup application scaling for multiple resources across multiple services in minutes.

Read More From URL:

https://aws.amazon.com/autoscaling/

158. True or False is an attribute of _____.

A. Binary

B. Boolean

C. Strings

D. Decimal

Answer: B

OFFICIAL EXPLANATION:

Boolean type attribute can have one of the two values namely, True or False. Use the BOOLEAN data type to store true and false values in a single-byte column. Regardless of the input string, a Boolean column stores and outputs "t" for true and "f" for false.

Read More From URL:

https://docs.aws.amazon.com/redshift/latest/dg/r_Boolean_ty pe.html

159. Which security feature is associated with a Subnet in a VPC to protect against Incoming traffic requests?

A. AWS Policy

B. NACL

C. Amazon HDK

D. Security Groups

Answer: B

OFFICIAL EXPLANATION:

A *network access control list (ACL)* is an optional layer of security for your VPC that acts as a firewall for controlling traffic in and out of one or more subnets. You might set up network ACLs with rules similar to your security groups in order to add an additional layer of security to your VPC.

Read More From URL:

https://docs.aws.amazon.com/vpc/latest/userguide/vpc-network-acls.html

160. A company wants to derive the costs for moving artefacts from on-premise to AWS, which must the consider?

A. AWS IAM

B. AWS Management console

C. AWS Cost Explorer

D. AWS TCO calculator

Answer: D

OFFICIAL EXPLANATION:

The AWS Documentation mentions the following Use this calculator to compare the cost of running your applications in an on-premises or colocation environment to AWS. Describe your on-premises or colocation configuration to produce a detailed cost comparison with AWS.

Read More From URL:

https://awstcocalculator.com/

161. Which of the following services creates and provisions AWS resources?

A. AWS CloudFormation

B. AWS Console

C. AWS Identity and Access Management

D. AWS CloudTrail

Answer: A

OFFICIAL EXPLANATION:

AWS CloudFormation refers to a service that creates and provisions your AWS resources AWS CloudFormation provides a common language for you to describe and provision all the infrastructure resources in your cloud environment. CloudFormation allows you to use a simple text file to model and provision, in an automated and secure manner, all the resources needed for your applications across all regions and accounts. This file serves as the single source of truth for your cloud environment.

Read More From URL:

https://aws.amazon.com/cloudformation/

162. Which Cloud Computing Model removes the need for your organization to manage the underlying infrastructure (usually hardware and operating systems) and allows you to focus on the deployment and management of your applications?

A. DaaS

B. CaaS

C. PaaS

D. Haas

Answer: C

OFFICIAL EXPLANATION:

Platforms as a service remove the need for organizations to manage the underlying infrastructure (usually hardware and operating systems) and allow you to focus on the deployment and management of your applications. This helps you be more efficient as you don't need to worry about resource procurement, capacity planning, software maintenance, patching, or any of the other undifferentiated heavy lifting involved in running your application.

Read More From URL:

https://aws.amazon.com/types-of-cloud-computing/

163. Which of the following is the responsibility of the customer when ensuring that data on EBS volumes is left safe

A. Deleting the data when the device is destroyed

B. Creating copies of EBS Volumes

C. Deleting EBS snapshots

D. Creating EBS snapshots

Answer: D

OFFICIAL EXPLANATION:

Creating snapshots of EBS Volumes can help ensure that you have a backup of your EBS volume in place.

Read More From URL:

https://docs.aws.amazon.com/AWSEC2/latest/UserGuide/EBSS
napshots.html

164. What offers profitable, resizable capacity for your databases?

A. Amazon DynamoDB

B. Amazon Relational Database Service

C. Amazon StaticDB

D. None of the above

Answers: B

OFFICIAL EXPLANATION:

Relational Database Service offers profitable, resizable capacity for your databases. Amazon Relational Database Service (Amazon RDS) makes it easy to set up, operate, and scale a relational database in the cloud. It provides cost-efficient and resizable capacity while automating time-consuming administration tasks such as hardware provisioning, database setup, patching and backups. It frees you to focus on your applications so you can give them the fast performance, high availability, security and compatibility they need.

Read More From URL:

https://aws.amazon.com/rds/

165. A company has launched an educational application that is intended for global usage. What service can help provide low latency access with best possible performance globally?

A. AWS CloudFront

B. AWS Route 53

C. AWS Cloudwatch

D. AWS Elastic bean stalk

Answer: A

OFFICIAL EXPLANATION:

Amazon CloudFront is a fast content delivery network (CDN) service that securely delivers data, videos, applications, and APIs to customers globally with low latency, high transfer speeds, all within a developer-friendly environment. CloudFront is integrated with AWS – both physical locations that are directly connected to the AWS global infrastructure, as well as other AWS services. CloudFront works seamlessly with services including AWS Shield for DDoS mitigation, Amazon S3, Elastic Load Balancing or Amazon EC2 as origins for your applications, and Lambda@Edge to run custom code closer to customers' users and to customize the user experience.

Read More From URL:

https://aws.amazon.com/cloudfront/

166. Which can be used to call AWS services from programming languages :

A. AWS SES
B. AWS HDK
C. AWS SDK
D. AWS SQS

Answer: C

The AWS SDK can be plugged in for various programming languages. Using the SDK you can then call the required AWS services.

Read More From URL:

https://aws.amazon.com/tools/

167. What is applied to a DB instance if you do not specify the desired parameter group while creating the instance?

A. Spot
B. Policy group

C. Parameter group

D. DynamoDB group

Answer: C

OFFICIAL EXPLANATION:

A parameter group is applied to a DB instance, if you do
not specify your desired parameter group while creating the
instance. A DB *parameter group* acts as a container for engine
configuration values that are applied to one or more DB instances.

If you create a DB instance without specifying a DB parameter
group, the DB instance uses a default DB parameter group. Each
default DB parameter group contains database engine defaults and
Amazon RDS system defaults based on the engine, compute class,
and allocated storage of the instance. You can't modify the
parameter settings of a default parameter group. Instead, you create
your own parameter group where you choose your own parameter
settings. Not all DB engine parameters can be changed in a
parameter group that you create.

Read More From URL:

https://docs.aws.amazon.com/AmazonRDS/latest/UserGuide/U
SER_WorkingWithParamGroups.html

168. What does S3 stand for?

A. Simple Storage Service

B. Simplified Storage Service

C. Simple Storage Service

D. Service for Static Storage

Answer: A

OFFICIAL EXPLANATION:

Amazon Simple Storage Service (Amazon S3) is an object storage service that offers industry-leading scalability, data availability, security, and performance. This means customers of all sizes and industries can use it to store and protect any amount of data for a range of use cases, such as websites, mobile applications, backup and restore, archive, enterprise applications, IoT devices, and big data analytics. Amazon S3 provides easy-to-use management features so you can organize your data and configure finely-tuned access controls to meet your specific business, organizational, and compliance requirements. Amazon S3 is designed for 99.999999999% (11 9's) of durability, and stores data for millions of applications for companies all around the world.

Read More From URL:

https://aws.amazon.com/s3/

169. If a company wants a secure way of using AWS API to call AWS services from EC2 Instances, which choice do you prefer?

A. IAM Users

B. AWS Console

C. IAM Policy

D. IAM Roles

Answer: D

OFFICIAL EXPLANATION:

The AWS Documentation mentions the following An IAM role is similar to a user, in that it is an AWS identity with permission policies that determine what the identity can and cannot do in AWS. However, instead of being uniquely associated with one person, a role is intended to be assumable by anyone who needs it. Also, a role does not have standard long-term credentials (password or access keys) associated with it. Instead, if a user assumes a role, temporary security credentials are created dynamically and provided to the user.

Read More From URL:

https://docs.aws.amazon.com/IAM/latest/UserGuide/id_roles.ht ml

170. Which of the following are 2 ways that AWS allows to link accounts?

A. Consolidating billing

B. TCO

C. AWS Organizations

D. Management console

Answer: A, C

OFFICIAL EXPLANATION:

The AWS Documentation mentions the following: You can use the consolidated billing feature in AWS Organizations to consolidate payment for multiple AWS accounts or multiple AISPL accounts. With consolidated billing, you can see a combined view of AWS charges incurred by all of your accounts. You also can get a cost report for each member account that is associated with your master account. Consolidated billing is offered at no additional charge.

Read More From URL:

https://docs.aws.amazon.com/awsaccountbilling/latest/aboutv2/consolidated-billing.html

171. How does Amazon maintain a synchronous reserved replica of that DB instance?

A. Tracking
B. Deployment
C. Placement
D. Development

Answer: B

OFFICIAL EXPLANATION:

Through this deployment option, Amazon maintains a synchronous reserved replica of that DB instance in another Availability Zone. AWS CodeDeploy is a fully managed deployment service that automates software deployments to a variety of compute services such as Amazon EC2, AWS Fargate, AWS Lambda, and your on-premises servers. AWS CodeDeploy makes it easier for you to rapidly release new features, helps you avoid downtime during application deployment, and handles the complexity of updating your applications. You can use AWS CodeDeploy to automate software deployments, eliminating the need for error-prone manual operations. The service scales to match your deployment needs.

Read More From URL:

https://aws.amazon.com/codedeploy/

172. Smith is working with a large data set, and he needs to import it into a relational database service. What AWS service will help him?

A. Amazon S3
B. Dynamodb
C. AWS EBS
D. RDS

Answer: D

OFFICIAL EXPLANATION:

Amazon Relational Database Service (Amazon RDS) makes it easy to set up, operate, and scale a relational database in the cloud. It provides cost-efficient and resizable capacity while automating time-consuming administration tasks such as hardware provisioning, database setup, patching and backups. It frees you to focus on your applications so you can give them the fast performance, high availability, security and compatibility they need.

.

Read More From URL:

https://aws.amazon.com/rds/

173. Which of the following helps in DDos protection. Choose 2 answers

A. Cloudfront

B. AWS CloudWatch

C. Aurora

D. AWS Shield

Answer: A, D

OFFICIAL EXPLANATION:

The AWS Documentation mentions the following on DDoS attacks One of the first techniques to mitigate DDoS attacks is to minimize the surface area that can be attacked thereby limiting the options for attackers and allowing you to build protections in a single place. We want to ensure that we do not expose our application or resources to ports, protocols or applications from where they do not expect any communication. Thus, minimizing the possible points of attack and letting us concentrate our mitigation efforts. In some cases, you can do this by placing your computation resources behind Content Distribution Networks

(CDNs) or Load Balancers and restricting direct Internet traffic to certain parts of your infrastructure like your database servers. In other cases, you can use firewalls or Access Control Lists (ACLs) to control what traffic.

Read More From URL:

https://aws.amazon.com/shield/ddos-attack-protection/

174. BBC Multitech wants a web application firewall in AWS , which can they make use of.?

A. AWS TCO

B. AWS Firewall

C. AWS WAF

D. AWS IAM

Answer: C

OFFICIAL EXPLANATION:

The AWS Documentation mentions the following AWS WAF is a web application firewall that lets you monitor the HTTP and https requests that are forwarded to Amazon CloudFront or an Application Load Balancer. AWS WAF also lets you control access to your content.

Read More From URL:

https://docs.aws.amazon.com/waf/latest/developerguide/waf-chapter.html

174. Which of the following is NOT true about an edge location?

A. Distribute content to users

B. Distribute load across multiple resources

C. Distribute load across one resources

D. Distribute keys to users

Answer: B

OFFICIAL EXPLANATION:

The AWS global infrastructure delivers a cloud infrastructure companies can depend on—no matter their size, changing needs, or challenges. The AWS Global Infrastructure is designed and built to deliver the most flexible, reliable, scalable, and secure cloud computing environment with the highest quality global network performance available today. Every component of the AWS infrastructure is design and built for redundancy and reliability, from regions to networking links to load balancers to routers and firmware using AWS Edge locations

Read More From URL:

https://aws.amazon.com/about-aws/global-infrastructure/

175. Which helps to add an extra layer of protection to the current authentication mechanism of user names and passwords for AWS?

A. Using multicode policy

B. Using a mix of passwords

C. Using MFA

D. Using AWS WAF

Answer: C

OFFICIAL EXPLANATION:

The AWS Documentation mentions the following AWS Multi-Factor Authentication (MFA) is a simple best practice that adds an extra layer of protection on top of your user name and password With MFA enabled, when a user signs in to an AWS website, they will be prompted for their user name and password (the first factor—what they know), as well as for an authentication code from their AWS MFA device (the second factor—what they have). Taken together, these multiple factors provide increased security for your AWS account settings and resources.

Read More From URL:

https://aws.amazon.com/iam/details/mfa/

176. The _____ service is targeted at organizations with multiple users or systems that use AWS products such as Amazon EC2, Amazon SimpleDB, and the AWS Management Console.

A. AWS Identity and Access Management

B. AWS Integrity Management

C. Amazon RDS

D. Amazon X-RAY

Answer: A

OFFICIAL EXPLANATION:

AWS Identity and Access Management (IAM) enables you to manage access to AWS services and resources securely. Using IAM, you can create and manage AWS users and groups, and use permissions to allow and deny their access to AWS resources.

IAM is a feature of your AWS account offered at no additional charge. You will be charged only for use of other AWS services by your users.

Read More From URL:

https://aws.amazon.com/iam/

177. Which of the following disaster recovery deployment mechanisms has the lowest downtime ?

A. Warm standby

B. Pilot light

C. Reboot

D. Dynamodb

Answer: A

OFFICIAL EXPLANATION:

The snapshot from the AWS Documentation shows the spectrum of the Disaster recovery methods. If you go to the further end of the spectrum you have the least time for downtime for the users.

Read More From URL:

https://aws.amazon.com/blogs/aws/new-whitepaper-use-aws-for-disaster-recovery/

178. Which of the following services in AWS allows for object level storage on the cloud?

A. Amazon S3

B. AWS MFA

C. Aurora

D. Amazon RDS

Answer: A

OFFICIAL EXPLANATION:

The AWS Documentation mentions the following Amazon S3 is object storage built to store and retrieve any amount of data from anywhere – web sites and mobile apps, corporate applications, and data from IoT sensors or devices. It is designed to deliver 99.999999999% durability, and stores data for millions of applications used by market leaders in every industry. For more information on Amazon S3, please refer to the below URL:

Read More From URL:

https://aws.amazon.com/s3/

179. Which of the following can be attached to EC2 Instances to store data?

A. Amazon EMR

B. Amazon EBS Snapshots

C. Amazon EBS Volumes

D. Amazon EBS Screenshots

Answer: C

OFFICIAL EXPLANATION:

The AWS Documentation mentions the following on EBS Volumes An Amazon EBS volume is a durable, block-level storage device that you can attach to a single EC2 instance. You can use EBS volumes as primary storage for data that requires frequent updates, such as the system drive for an instance or storage for a database application

Read More From URL:

https://docs.aws.amazon.com/AWSEC2/latest/UserGuide/EBS Volumes.html

180. Which supports the cloud design principle "design for failure and nothing will fail"?

A. Deploying an application in multiple Availability Zones

B. Deploying an application in one Availability Zones

C. Deploying an application in a single region

D. Using Amazon CloudWatch alerts to monitor performance

Answer: A

OFFICIAL EXPLANATION:

With instance status monitoring, you can quickly determine whether Amazon EC2 has detected any problems that might prevent your instances from running applications. Amazon EC2 performs automated checks on every running EC2 instance to identify hardware and software issues. You can view the results of these status checks to identify specific and detectable problems. This data augments the information that Amazon EC2 already provides about the intended state of each instance (such as pending, running, stopping) as well as the utilization metrics that Amazon CloudWatch monitors (CPU utilization, network traffic, and disk activity).

Read More From URL:

https://docs.aws.amazon.com/AWSEC2/latest/UserGuide/monitoring-system-instance-status-check.html

181. Which services allow the customer to retain full administrative privileges of the underlying virtual infrastructure?

A. Amazon IAM

B. Amazon EC2

C. Amazon EBS Snapshots

D. Amazon S3

Answer: B

OFFICIAL EXPLANATION:

Amazon Elastic Compute Cloud (Amazon EC2) is a web service that provides secure, resizable compute capacity in the cloud. It is designed to make web-scale cloud computing easier for developers.Amazon EC2's simple web service interface allows you to obtain and configure capacity with minimal friction. It provides you with complete control of your computing resources and lets you run on Amazon's proven computing environment. Amazon EC2 reduces the time required to obtain and boot new server instances to minutes, allowing you to quickly scale capacity, both up and down, as your computing requirements change. Amazon EC2 changes the economics of computing by allowing you to pay only for capacity that you actually use. Amazon EC2 provides developers the tools to build failure resilient applications and isolate them from common failure scenarios.

Read More From URL:

https://aws.amazon.com/ec2/

182.Suppose you want to host EC2 resources in the AWS Cloud, which networking component will you prefer?

A. AWS Trusted Advisor

B. AWS Autoscaling

C. AWS Elastic Load Balancer

D. AWS VPC.

Answer: D

OFFICIAL EXPLANATION:

The AWS Documentation mentions the following on Amazon VPC. Amazon Virtual Private Cloud (Amazon VPC) enables you to launch AWS resources into a virtual network that you've defined This virtual network closely resembles a traditional network that you'd operate in your own data center, with the benefits of using the scalable infrastructure of AWS.

Read More From URL:

https://docs.aws.amazon.com/AmazonVPC/latest/UserGuide/VPC_Introduction.html

183. Your company wants to use services which can be used to decouple resources hosted on the cloud. Which of the following services can help fulfil this requirement ?

A. AWS SES

B. AWS EBS Snapshots

C. AWS SQS

D. AWS Trusted Advisor

Answer: C

OFFICIAL EXPLANATION:

The AWS Documentation mentions the following on the Simple Queue Service Amazon Simple Queue Service (Amazon SQS) offers a reliable, highly-scalable hosted queue for storing messages as they travel between applications or microservices. It moves data between distributed application components and helps you decouple these components.

Read More From URL:

https://docs.aws.amazon.com/AWSSimpleQueueService/latest/S QSDeveloperGuide/Welcome.html

184.Which of the following services can help to analyze and process a large number of data sets?

A. AMAZON SQS

B. Amazon X-RAY

C. Amazon S3

D. EMR

Answer: D

OFFICIAL EXPLANATION:

Amazon EMR provides a managed Hadoop framework that makes it easy, fast, and cost-effective to process vast amounts of data across dynamically scalable Amazon EC2 instances. You can also run other popular distributed frameworks such as Apache Spark, HBase, Presto, and Flink in EMR, and interact with data in other AWS data stores such as Amazon S3 and Amazon DynamoDB. EMR Notebooks, based on the popular Jupyter Notebook, provide a development and collaboration environment for ad hoc querying and exploratory analysis.

Read More From URL:

https://aws.amazon.com/emr/

185. Jack is managing a web application running on the AWS Cloud which is currently utilizing eight EC2 servers for its compute platform. Earlier today, two of those web servers have been crashed. However, none of his customers were affected. What has Jack done correctly in this scenario?

A. Properly build a fault tolerant system.

B. Properly built a scalable system

C. Properly built an elastic system.

D. Properly built a fault involving system

Answer: A

OFFICIAL EXPLANATION:

Amazon EC2's simple web service interface allows you to obtain and configure capacity with minimal friction. It provides you with complete control of your computing resources and lets you run on Amazon's proven computing environment. Amazon EC2 reduces the time required to obtain and boot new server instances to minutes, allowing you to quickly scale capacity, both up and down, as your computing requirements change. Amazon EC2 changes the economics of computing by allowing you to pay only for capacity that you actually use. Amazon EC2 provides developers the tools to build failure resilient applications and isolate them from common failure scenarios.

Read More From URL:

https://aws.amazon.com/ec2/

186. Your company requires all the data on your EBS-backed EC2 volumes be encrypted. How would you go about doing this?

A. You cannot enable EBS encryption on a specific volume

B. Encryption can be done on the OS layer of the EBS volume

C. AWS allows you to encrypt the file system on an EBS volume on EBS volume setup

D. AWS allows you to decrypt the file system on an EBS volume on EBS volume setup

Answer: C

OFFICIAL EXPLANATION:

Amazon EBS encryption offers a simple encryption solution for your EBS volumes without the need to build, maintain, and secure your own key management infrastructure. When you create an encrypted EBS volume and attach it to a supported instance type, the following types of data are encrypted:

- Data at rest inside the volume
- All data moving between the volume and the instance
- All snapshots created from the volume
- All volumes created from those snapshots

Encryption operations occur on the servers that host EC2 instances, ensuring the security of both data-at-rest and data-in-transit between an instance and its attached EBS storage.

Read More From URL:

https://docs.aws.amazon.com/AWSEC2/latest/UserGuide/EBS Encryption.html

187. Which feature of RDS allows for data redundancy across regions and improves Disaster Recovery?

A. Multi-region replication
B. Multi-AZ
C. Creating Read Replicas
D. Deleting Read Replicas

Answer: C

OFFICIAL EXPLANATION:

Amazon RDS Read Replicas provide enhanced performance and durability for database (DB) instances. This feature makes it easy to elastically scale out beyond the capacity constraints of a single DB instance for read-heavy database workloads. You can create one or more replicas of a given source DB Instance and serve high-volume application read traffic from multiple copies of your data, thereby increasing aggregate read throughput. Read replicas can also be promoted when needed to become standalone DB instances. Read replicas are available in Amazon RDS for MySQL, MariaDB, PostgreSQL and Oracle as well as Amazon Aurora.

Read More From URL:

https://aws.amazon.com/rds/details/read-replicas/

We have taken care in preparing each question in the book., in spite of it if there are corrections to be made in the book please feel free to mail us at care@bigbangtechno.in . Our Architect will validate it and make the corresponding changes. After the changes are made, **we will publish your name with a 'Vote of Thanks' in Amazon Kindle Book Publish website.**

We hope you are satisfied with this book. **If you feel this book has helped you in some way for your preparation, please rate us 5 star in Amazon Kindle**. It will be a great moral support to us and will help us to improve the quality of the book in the forthcoming editions.

188.Which of the following is one of the benefits of AWS Security?

A. Scale Quickly

B. Starts manually once you upload your data.

C. Free for AWS premium members.

D. Scale slowly

Answer: A

OFFICIAL EXPLANATION:

Benefits of AWS Security

- **Keep Your Data Safe**: The AWS infrastructure puts strong safeguards in place to help protect your privacy. All data is stored in highly secure AWS data centers.

- **Meet Compliance Requirements**: AWS manages dozens of compliance programs in its infrastructure. This means that segments of your compliance have already been completed.

- **Save Money**: Cut costs by using AWS data centers. Maintain the highest standard of security without having to manage your own facility

- **Scale Quickly**: Security scales with your AWS Cloud usage. No matter the size of your business, the AWS infrastructure is designed to keep your data safe.

Read More From URL:

189. A company is planning to distribute contents to users across the globe. Which of the following components of the Cloudfront service would they use?

A. Amazon EBS Volumes

B. Amazon Edge locations

C. Amazon Availability Zones

D. Amazon Corner locations

Answer: B

OFFICIAL EXPLANATION:

The AWS global infrastructure delivers a cloud infrastructure companies can depend on—no matter their size, changing needs, or challenges. The AWS Global Infrastructure is designed and built to deliver the most flexible, reliable, scalable, and secure cloud computing environment with the highest quality global network performance available today. Every component of the AWS infrastructure is design and built for redundancy and reliability, from regions to networking links to load balancers to routers and firmware using AWS Edge locations

Read More From URL:

https://aws.amazon.com/about-aws/global-infrastructure/

191.Which of the following is one of the benefits of AWS Security?

A. Free for AWS premium members.

B. Scale Quickly

C. Scale Wise

D. Automatic encryption of all traffic

Answer: D

OFFICIAL EXPLANATION:

Automatic encryption of all traffic on the AWS global and regional networks between AWS secured facilities

Read More From URL:

https://aws.amazon.com/security/

192. A company is planning to distribute contents to users across the globe. Which of the following components of the Cloudfront service would they use?

A. Amazon SQS.

B. Amazon Availability Zones

C. Amazon Edge locations

D. Amazon Corner location

Answer: C

OFFICIAL EXPLANATION:

The AWS global infrastructure delivers a cloud infrastructure companies can depend on—no matter their size, changing needs, or challenges. The AWS Global Infrastructure is designed and built to deliver the most flexible, reliable, scalable, and secure cloud computing environment with the highest quality global network performance available today. Every component of the AWS infrastructure is design and built for redundancy and reliability, from regions to networking links to load balancers to routers and firmware using AWS Edge locations

Read More From URL:

https://aws.amazon.com/about-aws/global-infrastructure/

194. Considering Amazon EC2, which of the following is an advantage when it comes to the cost perspective?

A. The ability to pay nothing
B. The ability to choose low cost AMI's to prepare the EC2 Instances
C. Ability to tag instances to reduce the overall cost
D. The ability to only pay for what you use

Answer: D

OFFICIAL EXPLANATION:

One of the advantages of EC2 Instances is per second billing concept. This is given in the AWS documentation also, With per-second billing, you pay for only what you use. It takes cost of unused minutes and seconds in an hour off of the bill, so you can focus on improving your applications instead of maximizing usage to the hour. Especially, if you manage instances running for irregular periods of time, such as dev/testing, data processing, analytics, batch processing and gaming applications, can benefit.

Read More From URL:

https://aws.amazon.com/ec2/pricing/

195. Your company is planning on moving to the AWS Cloud Once the movement to the Cloud is complete, they want to ensure that the right security settings are put in place. Which of the below tools can assist from a Security compliance. Choose 2 answers from the options given below.

A. AWS Inspector
B. AWS TCO
C. AWS Groups
D. AWS Trusted Advisor

Answer: A, D

OFFICIAL EXPLANATION:

The AWS documentation mentions the following An online resource to help you reduce cost, increase performance, and improve security by optimizing your AWS environment, Trusted Advisor provides real time guidance to help you provision your resources following AWS best practices The AWS Inspector can inspect EC2 Instances against common threats.

Read More From URL:

https://aws.amazon.com/premiumsupport/trustedadvisor/

https://docs.aws.amazon.com/inspector/latest/userguide/inspect or_introduction.html

196. Which services can help to collect important metrics from AWS RDS and EC2 Instances.

A. Amazon CloudWatch

B. Amazon CloudSearch

C. Amazon CloudFormation

D. Amazon Cloud9

Answer: A

OFFICIAL EXPLANATION:

The AWS documentation mentions the following Amazon CloudWatch is a monitoring service for AWS cloud resources and the applications you run on AWS. You can use Amazon CloudWatch to collect and track metrics, collect and monitor log files, set alarms, and automatically react to changes in your AWS resources.

Read More From URL:

https://aws.amazon.com/cloudwatch/

197. A company wants a complete audit trail of all AWS services used within an account . In such a case which service can they use?

A. AWS Console

B. AWS Cloud Trail logs

C. ELASTIC BEAN STALK

D. Amazon EC2 instance usage report

Answer: B

OFFICIAL EXPLANATION:

Using Cloudwatch trail , one can monitor all the API activity conducted on all AWS services. The AWS Documentation additionally mentions the following AWS CloudTrail is a service that enables governance, compliance, operational auditing, and risk auditing of your AWS account. With CloudTrail, you can log, continuously monitor, and retain account activity related to actions across your AWS infrastructure. CloudTrail provides event history of your AWS account activity, including actions taken through the AWS Management Console, AWS SDKs, command line tools, and other AWS services. This event history simplifies security analysis, resource change tracking, and troubleshooting.

Read More From URL:

https://aws.amazon.com/cloudtrail/

198. Which service is most useful when a Disaster Recovery

method is triggered in AWS.

A. Amazon Config

B. Amazon EBS Volumes

C. Amazon Route 53

D. Amazon Inspector

Answer: C

OFFICIAL EXPLANATION:

Route53 is a domain name system service by AWS. When a Disaster does occur , it can be easy to switch to secondary sites using the Route53 service. The AWS Documentation additionally mentions the following Amazon Route 53 is a highly available and scalable cloud Domain Name System (DNS) web service. It is designed to give developers and businesses an extremely reliable and cost effective way to route end users to Internet applications by translating names like www.example.com into the numeric IP addresses like 192.0.2.1 that computers use to connect to each other. Amazon Route 53 is fully compliant with IPv6 as well.

Read More From URL:

https://aws.amazon.com/route53/

199. Which can be used to work with AWS services in a

programmatic manner

A. AWS IAM

B. AWS CLI

C. AWS Bash

D. AWS EBS Snapshots

Answer: B

OFFICIAL EXPLANATION:

It allows developers to easily work with the various AWS resources programmatically

Read More From URL:

https://aws.amazon.com/tools/

200. Currently your organization has an operational team that takes care of ID management in their on-premise data center. They now also need to manage users and groups created in AWS. Which of the following AWS tools would they need to use for performing this management function?

A. AWS Identity and Access Management (IAM)

B. AWS HDK

C. AWS Key Management Service (AWS KMS)

D. AWS SDK

Answer: A

OFFICIAL EXPLANATION:

The AWS documentation mentions the following AWS Identity and Access Management (IAM) is a web service that helps you securely control access to AWS resources. You use IAM to control who is authenticated (signed in) and authorized (has permissions) to use resources.

Read More From URL:

http://docs.aws.amazon.com/IAM/latest/UserGuide/introductio n.html

201. You have a devops team. They want to know if there is any service available in AWS which can be used to manage infrastructure as code. Which service can help them?

A. Using AWS Security Groups
B. Using AWS CloudWatch
C. Using AWS Cloudformation
D. Using AWS TCO

Answer: C

OFFICIAL EXPLANATION:

The AWS documentation mentions the following AWS CloudFormation is a service that helps you model and set up your Amazon Web Services resources so that you can spend less time managing those resources and more time focusing on your applications that run in AWS. You create a template that describes all the AWS resources that you want (like Amazon EC2 instances or Amazon RDS DB instances), and AWS CloudFormation takes care of provisioning and configuring those resources for you. You don't need to individually create and configure AWS resources and figure out what's dependent on what; AWS CloudFormation handles all of that

Read More From URL:

https://docs.aws.amazon.com/AWSCloudFormation/latest/User Guide/Welcome.html

202. Jonsnow wants a fully managed, petabyte-scale data warehouse service in the AWS cloud, which must he consider?

A. Amazon EC2

B. Amazon DynamoDB

C. Amazon Redshift

D. Amazon MongoDB

Answer: C

OFFICIAL EXPLANATION:

The AWS documentation mentions the following Amazon Redshift is a fully managed, petabyte-scale data warehouse service in the cloud. You can start with just a few hundred gigabytes of data and scale to a petabyte or more. This enables you to use your data to acquire new insights for your business and customers.

Read More From URL:

http://docs.aws.amazon.com/redshift/latest/mgmt/welcome.html

203. Choose the options which correctly mentions the responsibility of AWS according to the Shared Security Model? Choose 3 answers :

A. Securing edge locations

B. Managing Console

C. Monitoring physical device security

D. Implementing service organization Control (SOC) standards

Answer: A, C, D

OFFICIAL EXPLANATION:

The responsibility of AWS includes the following 1) Securing edge locations 2) Monitoring physical device security 3) Implementing service organization Control (SOC) standards

Read More From URL:

https://aws.amazon.com/compliance/shared-responsibility-model/

204. Helen's company want to get an idea on the costs being incurred so far for the resources being used in AWS. How can this be achieved?

A. By using TCO

B. By using the AWS Trusted Advisor dashboard This dashboard will give you all the costs.

C. By using the AWS Cost and Usage reports Explorer. Here you can see the running and forecast costs.

D. By seeing the AWS Cloud Watch logs.

Answer: C

OFFICIAL EXPLANATION:

The AWS documentation mentions the following on AWS Cost Reports Cost Explorer is a free tool that you can use to view your costs. You can view data up to the last 13 months, forecast how much you are likely to spend for the next three months, and get recommendations for what Reserved Instances to purchase

Read More From URL:

http://docs.aws.amazon.com/awsaccountbilling/latest/aboutv2/cost-explorer-what-is.html

205. Who has complete administrative control over all resources in the respective AWS account?

A. AWS IAM

B. AWS Technical Account Manager (TAM)

C. AWS User

D. AWS Account Owner

Answer: D

OFFICIAL EXPLANATION:

The entire of control of data within an AWS account is with the Account Owner.

Read More From URL:

http://docs.aws.amazon.com/general/latest/gr/acct-identifiers.html

206. Your design team wants to Reduce inter-dependencies so that failures do not impact other components while designing an application using AWS. Which of the following concepts does this requirement relate to?

A. Decoupling
B. Integration
C. Disintegration
D. Coupling

Answer: A

OFFICIAL EXPLANATION:

The entire concept of decoupling components is to ensure that the different components of an applications can be managed and maintained separately. If all components are tightly coupled then when one component goes down, the entire application would do down. Hence it is always a better design practice to decouple application components.

Read More From URL:

http://whatis.techtarget.com/definition/decoupled-architecture

207. If you want to increase the fault tolerance of an application, what will you do?.

A. Deploying resources across same edge locations

B. Deploying resources across one Availability Zones

C. Deploying resources across multiple edge locations

D. Deploying resources across multiple Availability Zones

Answer: D

OFFICIAL EXPLANATION:

Each AZ is a set of one or more data centers. By deploying your AWS resources to multiple Availability zones, you are designing with failure with mind So if one AZ were to go down, the other AZ's would still be up and running and hence your application would be more fault tolerant.

Read More From URL:

http://docs.aws.amazon.com/AmazonRDS/latest/UserGuide/Concepts.RegionsAndAvailabilityZones.html

208. Which of the following security requirements are managed by AWS? Select 3 answers :

A. Physical security

B. Primary and secondary passwords

C. Disk disposal

D. Hardware patching

Answer: A, C,D

OFFICIAL EXPLANATION:

As per the Shared Responsibility model , the Patching of the underlying hardware and physical security of AWS resources is the responsibility of AWS.

Read More From URL:

https://aws.amazon.com/compliance/shared-responsibility-model/

Disk disposal: Storage Device Decommissioning When a storage device has reached the end of its useful life, AWS procedures include a decommissioning process that is designed to prevent customer data from being exposed to unauthorized individuals. AWS uses the techniques detailed in DoD 5220.22-M ("National Industrial Security Program Operating Manual ") or NIST 800-88 ("Guidelines for Media Sanitization") to destroy data as part of the decommissioning process. All decommissioned magnetic storage devices are degaussed and physically destroyed in accordance with industry-standard practices

Read More From URL:

https://d0.awsstaticcom/whitepapers/aws-security-whitepaper.pdf

209. Choose the best term that relate to "Creating systems that scale to the required capacity based on changes in demand"

A. Departmentation

B. Elasticity

C. Decoupling

D. Coupling

Answer: B

OFFICIAL EXPLANATION:

The concept of Elasticity is the means of an application having the ability to scale up and scale down based on demand An example of such a service is the Autoscaling service.

Read More From URL:

https://aws.amazon.com/autoscaling/

210. What can be used to automate multiple AWS services through scripts?

A. AWS IAM

B. AWS EBS

C. AWS EC2

D. AWS CLI

Answer: D

OFFICIAL EXPLANATION:

The AWS Command Line Interface (CLI) is a unified tool to manage your AWS services. With just one tool to download and configure, you can control multiple AWS services from the command line and automate them through scripts.

Read More From URL:

https://aws.amazon.com/cli/

211.Which AWS network feature can help you make private connectivity between AWS and your premises data center?

A. AWS management Console

B. AWS Indirect Connect

C. AWS Direct Connect

D. AWS Fiber Connect

Answer: C

OFFICIAL EXPLANATION:

AWS Direct Connect is a cloud service solution that makes it easy to establish a dedicated network connection from your premises to AWS. Using AWS Direct Connect, you can establish private connectivity between AWS and your datacenter, office, or colocation environment, which in many cases can reduce your network costs, increase bandwidth throughput, and provide a more consistent network experience than Internet-based connections.

.

Read More From URL:

https://aws.amazon.com/directconnect/

212. SB Techies , a software company wants to analyze EC2

Instances against pre-defined security templates to check for vulnerabilities, which services can help them?

A. AWS Inspector

B. AWS Trusted Advisor

C. AWS SQS

D. AWS Policies

Answer: A

OFFICIAL EXPLANATION:

Amazon Inspector is an automated security assessment service that helps improve the security and compliance of applications deployed on AWS. Amazon Inspector automatically assesses applications for exposure, vulnerabilities, and deviations from best practices. After performing an assessment, Amazon Inspector produces a detailed list of security findings prioritized by level of severity. These findings can be reviewed directly or as part of detailed assessment reports which are available via the Amazon Inspector console or API.

Read More From URL:

https://aws.amazon.com/inspector/

213. Your application needs a storage layer to store artifacts such as photos and videos. Which of the following services can be used as the underlying storage mechanism?

A. Amazon EBS volume

B. Amazon Glacier

C. Aurora

D. Amazon S3

Answer: D

OFFICIAL EXPLANATION:

Amazon Simple Storage Service (Amazon S3) is an object storage service that offers industry-leading scalability, data availability, security, and performance. This means customers of all sizes and industries can use it to store and protect any amount of data for a range of use cases, such as websites, mobile applications, backup and restore, archive, enterprise applications, IoT devices, and big data analytics. Amazon S3 provides easy-to-use management features so you can organize your data and configure finely-tuned access controls to meet your specific business, organizational, and compliance requirements. Amazon S3 is designed for 99.999999999% (11 9's) of durability, and stores data for millions of applications for companies all around the world.

Read More From URL:

https://aws.amazon.com/s3/

214. Jill wants a storage mechanisms that can be used to store messages effectively across distributed systems, can you help him with this situation?

A. Amazon SES

B. AWS Console

C. Amazon SQS

D. Amazon EBS Volumes

Answer: C

OFFICIAL EXPLANATION:

Amazon Simple Queue Service (SQS) is a fully managed message queuing service that enables you to decouple and scale microservices, distributed systems, and serverless applications. SQS eliminates the complexity and overhead associated with managing and operating message oriented middleware, and empowers developers to focus on differentiating work. Using SQS, you can send, store, and receive messages between software components at any volume, without losing messages or requiring other services to be available. Get started with SQS in minutes using the AWS console, Command Line Interface or SDK of your choice, and three simple commands.

Read More From URL:

https://aws.amazon.com/sqs/

215 Choose the option which developers use to run Infrastructure as code?

A. AWS Accounts Manager

B. AWS CloudFormation

C. AWS User

D. AWS Cloud9

Answer: B

OFFICIAL EXPLANATION:

AWS CloudFormation provides a common language for you to describe and provision all the infrastructure resources in your cloud environment. CloudFormation allows you to use a simple text file to model and provision, in an automated and secure manner, all the resources needed for your applications across all regions and accounts. This file serves as the single source of truth for your cloud environment.

Read More From URL:

https://aws.amazon.com/cloudformation/

216.Your company is planning to offload some of the batch processing workloads that can be interrupted and resumed at any time. Which of the following instance types would be the most cost effective to use for this purpose?

A. Spot

B. On demand

C. Closed

D. Partial Upfront Reserved

Answer: A

OFFICIAL EXPLANATION:

The AWS documentation mentions the following Spot Instances are a cost-effective choice if you can be flexible about when your applications run and if your applications can be interrupted For example, Spot Instances are well-suited for data analysis, batch jobs, background processing, and optional tasks

Read More From URL:

http://docs.aws.amazon.com/AWSEC2/latest/UserGuide/using-spot-instances.html

217. The service which needs a user name and password to access AWS resources is?.

A. AWS CLI

B. AWS Management Console

C. AWS Software Development Kit (SDK)

D. AWS HDK

Answer: B

OFFICIAL EXPLANATION:

The AWS Management console allows you to access and manage Amazon Web Services through a simple and intuitive web-based user interface

Read More From URL:

https://aws.amazon.com/console/

218. Your company is planning to use the AWS Cloud , but there

is a management decision that resources need to split department wise. Which would help in effective management and also provide an efficient costing model towards managing multiple AWS account?.

A. Amazon Glacier

B. Amazon Dev Pay

C. DevOps

D. AWS organizations

Answer: D

OFFICIAL EXPLANATION:

The AWS Documentation mentions the following AWS Organizations offers policy-based management for multiple AWS accounts. With Organizations, you can create groups of accounts and then apply policies to those groups. Organizations enables you to centrally manage policies across multiple accounts, without requiring custom scripts and manual processes.

Read More From URL:

https://aws.amazon.com/organizations/

219. When logging into the AWS Console, which can be used as an additional layer of security to using a user name and password ?

A. Root Denied privileges

B. Tertiary password

C. Multi-Factor Authentication (MFA)

D. Primary user name

Answer: C

OFFICIAL EXPLANATION:

The AWS Documentation mentions the following AWS Multi-Factor Authentication (MFA) is a simple best practice that adds an extra layer of protection on top of your user name and password.

Read More From URL:

https://aws.amazon.com/iam/details/mfa/

220. YYY company wants a quick deployment of resources and use different programming languages such as .Net and Java. Which AWS service does this?

A. AWS Elastic Compute Cloud (Amazon EC2)

B. AWS Elastic Beanstalk

C. AWS Cloudformation

D. AWS CloudTrail

Answer: B

OFFICIAL EXPLANATION:

The AWS Documentation mentions the following AWS Elastic Beanstalk is an easy-to-use service for deploying and scaling web applications and services developed with Java, .NET, PHP, Node.js, Python, Ruby, Go, and Docker on familiar servers such as Apache, Nginx, Passenger, and IIS.

Read More From URL:

https://aws.amazon.com/elasticbeanstalk/?p=tile

221. Nike handles a crucial ecommerce application and needs to have an uptime of at least 99.5%. He makes a decision to move the application to the AWS Cloud. Which of the following deployment strategies can help build a robust architecture for such an application in AWS?

A. Deploying the application across many Availability zones

B. Deploying the application across multiple keywords

C. Deploying the application across one region

D. Deploying the application across multiple Regions

Answer: D

OFFICIAL EXPLANATION:

The AWS Documentation mentions the following Businesses are using the AWS cloud to enable faster disaster recovery of their critical IT systems without incurring the infrastructure expense of a second physical site. The AWS cloud supports many popular disaster recovery (DR) architectures from "pilot light" environments that may be suitable for small customer workload data center failures to "hot standby" environments that enable rapid failover at scale. With data centers in Regions all around the world, AWS provides a set of cloud-based disaster recovery services that enable rapid recovery of your IT infrastructure and data.

Read More From URL:

https://aws.amazon.com/disaster-recovery/

222. When IT companies host resources on the AWS Cloud, which reduces the overall expenditure for them?

A. They continually reduce the cost of cloud computing

B. They periodically reduce the cost of cloud computing

C. They don't deploy multiple resources

D. They have poor secondary security

Answer: A

OFFICIAL EXPLANATION:

The AWS Documentation mentions the following AWS continues to lower the cost of cloud computing for its customers. In 2014, AWS has reduced the cost of compute by an average of 30%, storage by an average of 51% and relational databases by an average of 28%. AWS continues to drive down the cost of your IT infrastructure

Read More From URL:

https://aws.amazon.com/economics/learn-more/

223. Emma is planning on deploying a video based application onto the AWS Cloud. Which of the below services can help stream the content in an efficient manner to all the users across the globe?

A. Amazon EC2

B. Amazon CloudFront

C. Amazon CloudWatchl

D. Amazon Config

Answer: B

OFFICIAL EXPLANATION:

The AWS Documentation mentions the following Amazon CloudFront is a web service that gives businesses and web application developers an easy and cost effective way to distribute content with low latency and high data transfer speeds. Like other AWS services, Amazon CloudFront is a self-service, pay-per-use offering, requiring no long term commitments or minimum fees. With CloudFront, your files are delivered to end-users using a global network of edge locations.

Read More From URL:

https://aws.amazon.com/cloudfront/

224. Can you suggest any one fully managed NoSQL database service available in AWS?

A. AWS MongoDB

B. AWS MFA

C. AWS CLI

D. AWS DynamoDB

Answer: D

OFFICIAL EXPLANATION:

The AWS Documentation mentions the following Amazon DynamoDB is a fast and flexible NoSQL database service for all applications that need consistent, single-digit millisecond latency at any scale. It is a fully managed cloud database and supports both document and key-value store models. Its flexible data model, reliable performance, and automatic scaling of throughput capacity, makes it a great fit for mobile, web, gaming, ad tech, IoT, and many other applications.

https://aws.amazon.com/dynamodb/

225. Suppose you want all of your AWS resources to be available the majority of the time, which option will suit this?

A. Use Route 53 health checking to configure Active-Active Failover.

B. Use RDS health checking to configure Passive -Active Failover.

C. Use Route 53 health checking to configure Active-Passive Failover.

D. Use RDS health checking to configure Passive-Passive Failover.

Answer: A

OFFICIAL EXPLANATION:

Use **Active-Active** failover configuration when you want all of your resources to be available the majority of the time. When a resource becomes unavailable, Route 53 can detect that it's unhealthy and stop including it when responding to queries.

.

Read More From URL:

https://docs.aws.amazon.com/Route53/latest/DeveloperGuide/dns-failover-types.html

226. What rules must be followed regarding the bucket name when you create an S3 bucket,? (Select all that apply)

A. Bucket names must contain uppercase and lowercase letters.
B. Bucket names must be between 3-63 characters in length.
C. Bucket names can be formatted as a Physical address.
D. Bucket name must be unique across all of AWS.

Answer: B D

OFFICIAL EXPLANATION:

Amazon S3 provides APIs for creating and managing buckets. By default, you can create up to 100 buckets in each of your AWS accounts. If you need more buckets, you can increase your account bucket limit to a maximum of 1,000 buckets by submitting a service limit increase.

Read More From URL:

https://docs.aws.amazon.com/AmazonS3/latest/dev/UsingBucke t.html

227. What tool can you recommend so they can do a cost benefit analysis of moving to the AWS Cloud . They are very concerned about how much it will cost once their entire I.T. infrastructure is running on AWS.?

A. AWS MFA

B. AWS Estimate Calculator

C. AWS Management console

D. AWS TCO calculator

Answer: D

OFFICIAL EXPLANATION:

AWS helps you reduce Total Cost of Ownership (TCO) by reducing the need to invest in large capital expenditures and providing a pay-as-you-go model that empowers you to invest in the capacity you need and use it only when the business requires it.

Read More From URL:

https://aws.amazon.com/tco-calculator/

228. Jacqueline has created a web application, placing it's underlining infrastructure in the N. Virginia (US-East-1) region.

After several months, Jacqueline notices that much of the traffic coming to her website is coming from Japan. What can Jacqueline do to (best) help reduce latency for her users in Japan?

A. Change to a Indian hosting service.

B. Delete the website content.

C. Create a CDN using CloudFront, making sure the proper content is cached at Edge Locations closest to Japan.

D. Block the traffic using Traffic controller

Answer: C

OFFICIAL EXPLANATION:

The AWS global infrastructure delivers a cloud infrastructure companies can depend on—no matter their size, changing needs, or challenges. The AWS Global Infrastructure is designed and built to deliver the most flexible, reliable, scalable, and secure cloud computing environment with the highest quality global network performance available today. Every component of the AWS infrastructure is design and built for redundancy and reliability, from regions to networking links to load balancers to routers and firmware using AWS Edge locations

Read More From URL:

https://aws.amazon.com/about-aws/global-infrastructure/

229. Which of the following is used for a drag-and-drop interface to edit cloudFormation templates?

A. CloudFormation Designer

B. CloudFormation opener

C. CloudFormation Editor

D. CloudFormation creator

Answer: A

OFFICIAL EXPLANATION:

AWS CloudFormation Designer (Designer) is a graphic tool for creating, viewing, and modifying AWS CloudFormation templates. With Designer, you can diagram your template resources using a drag-and-drop interface, and then edit their details using the integrated JSON and YAML editor. Whether you are a new or an experienced AWS CloudFormation user, AWS CloudFormation Designer can help you quickly see the interrelationship between a template's resources and easily modify templates.

Read More From URL:

https://docs.aws.amazon.com/AWSCloudFormation/latest/User Guide/working-with-templates-cfn-designer.html

230. Which term best suits to "Creating systems that scale to the required capacity based on changes on demand"?

A. Elasticity

B. Coupling

C. Decoupling

D. Rigidity

Answer: A

OFFICIAL EXPLANATION:

Amazon EC2 Auto Scaling helps you ensure that you have the correct number of Amazon EC2 instances available to handle the load for your application. You create collections of EC2 instances, called *Auto Scaling groups*. You can specify the minimum number of instances in each Auto Scaling group, and Amazon EC2 Auto Scaling ensures that your group never goes below this size. You can specify the maximum number of instances in each Auto Scaling group, and Amazon EC2 Auto Scaling ensures that your group never goes above this size. If you specify the desired capacity, either when you create the group or at any time thereafter, Amazon EC2 Auto Scaling ensures that your group has this many instances. If you specify scaling policies, then Amazon EC2 Auto Scaling can launch or terminate instances as demand on your application increases or decreases.

Read More From URL:

https://docs.aws.amazon.com/autoscaling/ec2/userguide/what-is-amazon-ec2-auto-scaling.html

231.The most important principles when designing cloud based systems are _____ and _____ ?

A. Assume everything will fail and Build loosely-coupled

components

B. Use as many services as possible and Build Tightly-coupled components

C. Build Tightly-coupled components and Build loosely-coupled components

D. Build loosely-coupled components and Use as many services as possible

Answer: A

OFFICIAL EXPLANATION:

See more from the screenshots in the website.

Read More From URL:

https://aws.amazon.com/architecture/

232. Which of the following could you use beside DynamoDB which lets you focus on building great applications for your customers without worrying about performance at scale?

A. DynamoDB SDK

B. DynamoDB CLI

C. DynamoDB DAX

D. All of the above

Answer: C

OFFICIAL EXPLANATION:

Amazon DynamoDB Accelerator (DAX) is a fully managed, highly available, in-memory cache for DynamoDB that delivers up to a 10x performance improvement – from milliseconds to microseconds – even at millions of requests per second. DAX does all the heavy lifting required to add in-memory acceleration to your DynamoDB tables, without requiring developers to manage cache invalidation, data population, or cluster management. Now you can focus on building great applications for your customers without worrying about performance at scale. You do not need to modify application logic, since DAX is compatible with existing DynamoDB API calls. You can enable DAX with just a few clicks in the AWS Management Console or using the AWS SDK. Just as with DynamoDB, you only pay for the capacity you provision

Read More From URL:

https://aws.amazon.com/dynamodb/dax/

233. An organization wants to move to Cloud and are looking for a secure encrypted database storage option. Which of the below mentioned AWS functionalities helps them to achieve this?

A. AWS EC2 dashboard
B. Single-tier encryption with VPC.
C. Multi-tier encryption with VPC.
D. AWS EBS encryption

Answer: D

OFFICIAL EXPLANATION:

Amazon EBS encryption offers a simple encryption solution for your EBS volumes without the need to build, maintain, and secure your own key management infrastructure. When you create an encrypted EBS volume and attach it to a supported instance type, the following types of data are encrypted:

- Data at rest inside the volume
- All data moving between the volume and the instance
- All snapshots created from the volume
- All volumes created from those snapshots

Encryption operations occur on the servers that host EC2 instances, ensuring the security of both data-at-rest and data-in-transit between an instance and its attached EBS storage.

Read More From URL:

https://docs.aws.amazon.com/AWSEC2/latest/UserGuide/EBS Encryption.html

234. Anne's company wants a service which is a compatible PostgreSQL database which also has the ability to grow in storage size on its own. What can she prefer?

A. AWS HDK

B. MongoDB

C. Aurora

D. RDS PostgreSQL

Answer: C

OFFICIAL EXPLANATION:

Amazon Aurora is a MySQL and PostgreSQL-compatible relational database built for the cloud, that combines the performance and availability of traditional enterprise databases with the simplicity and cost-effectiveness of open source databases.

Amazon Aurora is up to five times faster than
standard MySQL databases and three times faster than standard
PostgreSQL databases. It provides the security, availability, and
reliability of commercial databases at 1/10th the cost. Amazon
Aurora is fully managed by Amazon Relational Database Service
(RDS), which automates time-consuming administration tasks like
hardware provisioning, database setup, patching, and backups.

Read More From URL:

https://aws.amazon.com/rds/aurora/

234. A S3 storage class that would be ideal for storing thumbnails, transcoded media, or other processed data that can be easily reproduced is known as?

A. S3 Slow Access class
B. S3 Reduced Redundancy Storage
C. S3 Rapid Access Class
D. S3 Increased redundancy storage

Answer: B

OFFICIAL EXPLANATION:

Reduced Redundancy Storage (RRS) is an Amazon S3 storage option that enables customers to store noncritical, reproducible data at lower levels of redundancy than Amazon S3's standard storage. It provides a highly available solution for distributing or sharing content that is durably stored elsewhere, or for storing thumbnails, transcoded media, or other processed data that can be easily reproduced. The RRS option stores objects on multiple devices across multiple facilities, providing 400 times the durability of a typical disk drive, but does not replicate objects as many times as standard Amazon S3 storage.

Read More From URL:

https://aws.amazon.com/s3/reduced-redundancy/

235. The best option when you want to store archive data is ?

A. Amazon Storage Gateway

B. Amazon EC2

C. Amazon Glacier

D. Amazon SQS

Answer: C

OFFICIAL EXPLANATION:

The AWS Documentation mentions the following Amazon Glacier is a secure, durable, and extremely low-cost cloud storage service for data archiving and long-term backup. It is designed to deliver 99.999999999% durability, and provides comprehensive security and compliance capabilities that can help meet even the most stringent regulatory requirements.

Read More From URL:

https://aws.amazon.com/glacier/

236. Which of the following would you utilize to ensure costs are minimized , if there is a requirement to host EC2 Instances in the AWS Cloud wherein the utilization is guaranteed to be consistent for a long period of time?

A. Full upfront reserved instances

B. On-demand instances

C. Reserved instances

D. Partial upfront reserved instances

Answer: C

OFFICIAL EXPLANATION:

When you have instances that will be used continuously and throughout the year, the best option is to buy reserved instances. By buying reserved instances, you are actually allocated an instance for the entire year or the duration you specify with a reduced cost.

Read More From URL:

https://aws.amazon.com/ec2/pricing/reserved-instances/

237. Kile's company wants a dedicated connection from on-premise infrastructure to resources hosted in the AWS Cloud. What service can be utilized?

A. AWS Direct Connect

B. AWS Policies

C. AWS Indirect connect

D. AWS Subnets

Answer: A

OFFICIAL EXPLANATION:

The AWS Documentation mentions the following AWS Direct Connect makes it easy to establish a dedicated network connection from your premises to AWS. Using AWS Direct Connect, you can establish private connectivity between AWS and your datacenter, office, or colocation environment, which in many cases can reduce your network costs, increase bandwidth throughput, and provide a more consistent network experience than Internet-based connections.

Read More From URL:

https://aws.amazon.com/directconnect/?p=tile

238. A category recommendation which is not given by the AWS Trusted Advisor?

A. Groups

B. Low availability

C. Cost Optimization

D. Discipline

E. High Availability

Answer: E

OFFICIAL EXPLANATION:

Screenshot in AWS Doc shows what services the Trusted Advisor Dashboard offers.

Read More From URL:

https://aws.amazon.com/premiumsupport/trustedadvisor/

239. A company is deploying an application that needs a storage layer to store artefacts such as photos and videos. Which of the following services can be used as the underlying storage mechanism?.

A. Amazon EBS volume

B. Amazon EC2

C. Amazon S3

D. Aurora

Answer: C

OFFICIAL EXPLANATION:

Amazon S3 is the default storage service that should be considered for companies. If provides durable storage for all static content.

Read More From URL:

https://aws.amazon.com/s3/

240. When granting permissions to users via the AWS Identity and Access Management tool, which principles should be applied ?

A. Principle of poorest privilege

B. Principle of least privilege

C. Principle of most privilege

D. Principle of medium privilege

Answer: B

OFFICIAL EXPLANATION:

The principle means giving a user account only those privileges which are essential to perform its intended function. For example, a user account for the sole purpose of creating backups does not need to install software: hence, it has rights only to run backup and backup-related applications

Read More From URL:

https://en.wikipedia.org/wiki/Principle_of_least_privilege

241. A service which is equivalent to hosting virtual servers on an on-premise location is ?

A. AWS EC2

B. AWS MFA

C. AWS TCO

D. AWS Availability zones

Answer: A

OFFICIAL EXPLANATION:

The AWS Documentation mentions the following Amazon Elastic Compute Cloud (Amazon EC2) is a web service that provides secure, resizable compute capacity in the cloud It is designed to make web-scale cloud computing easier for developers.

Read More From URL:

https://aws.amazon.com/ec2/

242. You have a set of EC2 Instances hosted on the AWS Cloud and you get a DDos attack from the internet. At such a time which of the following can help in reducing the overall threat to your EC2 Instances? Choose 2 answers from the options given below

A. Usage of Security Groups

B. Usage of AWS Cloudformation

C. Usage of Network Access Control Lists

D. Usage of the policies

Answer: A, C

OFFICIAL EXPLANATION:

The AWS Documentation mentions the following A security group acts as a virtual firewall for your instance to control inbound and outbound traffic A network access control list (ACL) is an optional layer of security for your VPC. that acts as a firewall for controlling traffic in and out of one or more subnets.

Read More From URL:

https://docs.aws.amazon.com/AmazonVPC/latest/UserGuide/V
PC_SecurityGroups.html

Read More From URL:

https://docs.aws.amazon.com/AmazonVPC/latest/UserGuide/V
PC_ACLs.html

243.Which of the following can be used to spin up EC2 instances
on the AWS Cloud when your company is using VM Templates?

A. AWS Cloud9

B. Amazon Machines Images

C. Amazon ABS Screenshots

D. Amazon VMware

Answer: B

OFFICIAL EXPLANATION:

The AWS Documentation mentions the following An Amazon
Machine Image (AMI) provides the information required to launch
an instance, which is a virtual server in the cloud. You specify an
AMI when you launch an instance, and you can launch as many
instances from the AMI as you need. You can also launch instances
from as many different AMIs as you need

Read More From URL:

https://docs.aws.amazon.com/AWSEC2/latest/UserGuide/AMIs
.html

244. Choose one of the option that cannot be used to get data onto Amazon Glacier.

A. AWS SQS

B. AWS S3 Lifecycle policies

C. AWS Glacier SDK

D. AWS console

Answer: D

OFFICIAL EXPLANATION:

Note that the AWS Console cannot be used to upload data onto Glacier. The console can only be used to create a Glacier vault which can be used to upload the data.

Read More From URL:

https://docs.aws.amazon.com/amazonglacier/latest/dev/uploadin g-an-archive.html

245. Your company has the following requirements as far as the support plan goes 24x7 access to Cloud Support Engineers via email, chat & phone, a response time of less than 1 hour for any critical faults Which of the following plans will suffice keeping in mind the cost factor.

A. Enterprise

B. Department

C. Spot

D. Basic

Answer: A

OFFICIAL EXPLANATION:

The Enterprise support plan has support time less than 15 minutes for Business-critical system down.

Read More From URL:

https://aws.amazon.com/premiumsupport/compare-plans/

246. Select the options which are features of an edge location. Choose 3 answers from the options given below

A. Distribute content to users

B. Cache common responses

C. Distribute load along some resources

D. Used in conjunction with the Cloudfront service

Answer: A, B, D

OFFICIAL EXPLANATION:

The AWS Documentation mentions the following Amazon CloudFront employs a global network of edge locations and regional edge caches that cache copies of your content close to your viewers. Amazon CloudFront ensures that end-user requests are served by the closest edge location. As a result, viewer requests travel a short distance, improving performance for your viewers. For files not cached at the edge locations and the regional edge caches, Amazon CloudFront keeps persistent connections with your origin servers so that those files can be fetched from the origin servers as quickly as possible.

Read More From URL:

https://aws.amazon.com/cloudfront/details/

247. MLM company wants a Lifecycle policies that can be used to move objects to archive storage., which can be used?

A. AWS TCO

B. Aurora

C. Amazon S3

D. Amazon SDK

Answer: C

OFFICIAL EXPLANATION:

The AWS Documentation mentions the following Lifecycle configuration enables you to specify the lifecycle management of objects in a bucket. The configuration is a set of one or more rules, where each rule defines an action for Amazon S3 to apply to a group of objects. These actions can be classified as follows: • Transition actions – In which you define when objects transition to another storage class. For example, you may choose to transition objects to the STANDARD_IA (IA, for infrequent access) storage class 30 days after creation, or archive objects to the GLACIER storage class one year after creation. • Expiration actions – In which you specify when the objects expire. Then Amazon S3 deletes the expired objects on your behalf.

Read More From URL:

https://aws.amazon.com/s3/

248. Amazon RDS allows for better availability of databases. Choose 2 answers from the options given below which justifies the above statement:

A. AWS CLI

B. Multi-AZ

C. Read Replica's

D. Single-Region

Answer: B, C

OFFICIAL EXPLANATION:

The AWS Documentation mentions the following If you are looking to use replication to increase database availability while protecting your latest database updates against unplanned outages, consider running your DB instance as a Multi-AZ deployment. You can use Multi-AZ deployments and Read Replicas in conjunction to enjoy the complementary benefits of each. You can simply specify that a given Multi-AZ deployment is the source DB instance for your Read Replica(s). That way you gain both the data durability and availability benefits of Multi-AZ deployments and the read scaling benefits of Read Replicas.

Read More From URL:

https://aws.amazon.com/ec2/pricing/reserved-instances/

249. Which of the following types of instances should be chosen to be cost effective if there is a requirement hosting a set of servers in the Cloud for a short period of 6 months?

A. Full upfront cots reserved

B. Partial Upfront costs Reserved

C. Reserved instances

D. On-Demand

Answer: D

OFFICIAL EXPLANATION:

Since the requirement is just for 3 months, then the best cost effective option is to use On-Demand Instances.

Read More From URL:

https://aws.amazon.com/ec2/pricing/on-demand/

250. A company wants to transfer petabytes of data from on-premise locations to the AWS Cloud, how can they do it?

A. AWS Import/Export

B. AWS MFA

C. AWS Snowball

D. AWS Transfer

Answer: C

OFFICIAL EXPLANATION:

The AWS Documentation mentions the following Snowball is a petabyte-scale data transport solution that uses secure appliances to transfer large amounts of data into and out of the AWS cloud Using Snowball addresses common challenges with large-scale data transfers including high network costs, long transfer times, and security concerns. Transferring data with Snowball is simple, fast, secure, and can be as little as one-fifth the cost of high-speed Internet.

Read More From URL:

https://aws.amazon.com/snowball/?p=tile

251. When working with the AWS Cloud what are the major advantage? Choose 2 answers from the options given below.

A. Having no control over the physical infrastructure, so you don't need to worry about what AWS is doing.

B. Having the pay as you go model, so you don't need to worry if you are burning costs for non-running resources.

C. No Upfront costs

D. More upfront costs

Answer: B, C

OFFICIAL EXPLANATION:

With AWS, some of the benefits you have is the "Pay as you go model" and not having the need to pay upfront for using AWS resources.

Read More From URL:

https://aws.amazon.com/application-hosting/benefits/

252. Hannah wants to move an existing Oracle database to the AWS Cloud , how can she do it?

A. AWS Database Migration Service

B. AWS Cloud9

C. AWS TCO

D. AWS Trusted Advisor

Answer: A

OFFICIAL EXPLANATION:

The AWS Documentation mentions the following AWS Database Migration Service helps you migrate databases to AWS quickly and securely. The source database remains fully operational during the migration, minimizing downtime to applications that rely on the database. The AWS Database Migration Service can migrate your data to and from most widely used commercial and open-source databases.

Read More From URL:

https://aws.amazon.com/dms/

253. AWS RDS allows for offloading reads of the database using which of the following feature?

A. Deleting read replicas

B. Storing read replicas

C. Creating Read Replica's

D. Using Single-AZ feature

Answer: C

OFFICIAL EXPLANATION:

The AWS Documentation mentions the following You can reduce the load on your source DB Instance by routing read queries from your applications to the read replica. Read replicas allow you to elastically scale out beyond the capacity constraints of a single DB instance for read-heavy database workloads.

Read More From URL:

https://aws.amazon.com/rds/details/read-replicas/

254. Another geographic location in AWS refers to what?

A. Region

B. Data Point

C. Availability Zone

D. Corner location

Answer: A

OFFICIAL EXPLANATION:

Regions correspond to different geographic locations in AWS.

Read More From URL:

https://docs.aws.amazon.com/AmazonRDS/latest/UserGuide/C oncepts.RegionsAndAvailabilityZones.html

255. BBC company wants to have a database hosted on AWS and they want to have control over the database itself. How can they do it?

A. Using the AWS DynamoDB service

B. Using the AWS EBS services

C. Hosting on the database on an EC2 Instance

D. Using the MongoDB service

Answer: C

OFFICIAL EXPLANATION:

If you want a self-managed database, that means you want complete control over the database engine and the underlying infrastructure. In such a case you need to host the database on an EC2 Instance

Read More From URL:

https://aws.amazon.com/ec2/

256. A company currently has an application which consist of a .Net layer which connects to a MySQL database. They now want to

move this application onto AWS. Which of the following would be an ideal database in AWS to migrate to for high availability?

A. An EC2 instance with MySQL installed.

B. StaticDB

C. Aurora

D. An EC2 instance with NoSQL installed

Answer: C

OFFICIAL EXPLANATION:

The AWS Documentation mentions the following Amazon Aurora (Aurora) is a fully managed, MySQL- and PostgreSQL-compatible, relational database engine. It combines the speed and reliability of high-end commercial databases with the simplicity and cost-effectiveness of open-source databases. It delivers up to five times the throughput of MySQL and up to three times the throughput of PostgreSQL without requiring changes to most of your existing applications.

Read More From URL:

https://docs.aws.amazon.com/AmazonRDS/latest/UserGuide/A uroraOverview.html

257. Choose 2 answers from the options given below that are NOT TRUE when it comes to elasticity.

A. Diverting traffic to instances based on the users

B. Diverting traffic to instances with the least load

C. Diverting traffic across multiple regions

D. Diverting traffic to instances with higher capacity

Answer: C, D

OFFICIAL EXPLANATION:

The concept of Elasticity is the means of an application having the ability to scale up and scale down based on demand. An example of such a service is the Autoscaling service.

Read More From URL:

https://aws.amazon.com/autoscaling/

258. "Distributing traffic to multiple EC2 Instances" relates to :

A. EBS Volumes

B. Subnets

C. Aurora

D. Elastic Load Balancer

Answer: D

OFFICIAL EXPLANATION:

The AWS Documentation mentions the following A load balancer distributes incoming application traffic. across multiple EC2 instances in multiple Availability Zones. This increases the fault tolerance of your applications. Elastic Load Balancing detects unhealthy instances and routes traffic only to healthy instances.

Read More From URL:

https://docs.aws.amazon.com/elasticloadbalancing/latest/classic/introduction.html

259. "Scaling up resources based on demand", this statement means

A. Glacier

B. Elastic Load Balancer

C. Manual scaling

D. Auto Scaling

Answer: D

OFFICIAL EXPLANATION:

The AWS Documentation mentions the following AWS Auto Scaling monitors your applications and automatically adjusts capacity to maintain steady, predictable performance at the lowest possible cost. Using AWS Auto Scaling, it's easy to setup application scaling for multiple resources across multiple services in minutes.

Read More From URL:

https://aws.amazon.com/autoscaling/

260. A company is planning to migrate their existing AWS Services to the Cloud. Which of the following would help them do a cost benefit analysis of moving to the AWS Cloud ?

A. AWS management console

B. AWS TCO calculator

C. AWS Security groups

D. AWS Consolidating billing

Answer: B

OFFICIAL EXPLANATION:

The AWS Documentation mentions the following Use this calculator to compare the cost of running your applications in an on-premises or colocation environment to AWS. Describe your on-premises or colocation configuration to produce a detailed cost comparison with AWS.

Read More From URL:

https://awstcocalculator.com/

261. How does AWS perform on its behalf for EBS volumes to make it less probe to failure?

A. Replication of the volume across different Availability Zones

B. Replication of the volume in the same Availability Zone

C. Deploying of the volume across Regions

D. Deploying of the volume across Edge locations

Answer: B

OFFICIAL EXPLANATION:

When you create an EBS volume in an Availability Zone, it is automatically replicated within that zone to prevent data loss due to failure of any single hardware component

Read More From URL:

https://docs.aws.amazon.com/AWSEC2/latest/UserGuide/EBS Volumes.html

262. .NET calls AWS using which of the following services

A. AWS SDK

B. AWS CLI

C. AWS MFA

D. AWS HDK

Answer: A

OFFICIAL EXPLANATION:

The AWS SDK can be plugged in for various programming languages. Using the SDK you can then call the required AWS services.

Read More From URL:

https://aws.amazon.com/tools/

263.In order to predict the cost of moving resources from on-premise to the cloud, which of the following can be used ?

A. AWS Migration

B. AWS TCO

C. AWS Cost explorer

D. AWS MFA

Answer: B

OFFICIAL EXPLANATION:

Use TCO calculator to compare the cost of your applications in an on-premises or traditional hosting environment to AWS. Describe your on-premises or hosting environment configuration to produce a detailed cost comparison with AWS.

Read More From URL:

https://aws.amazon.com/tco-calculator/

264. What is the basic concept of an AWS region?

A. It is a geographical area divided into Availability Zones

B. It is a geographical area divided into regions

C. It is a collection of Corner locations

D. It is the same as an Availability zone

Answer: A

OFFICIAL EXPLANATION:

A region is a geographical area divided into Availability Zones. Each region contains at least two Availability Zones.

Read More From URL:

https://docs.aws.amazon.com/AWSEC2/latest/UserGuide/using
-regions-availability-zones.html

265. Choose 3 answers from the options given below . In AWS, which security aspects are the customer's responsibility?

A. Security Group and ACL (Access Control List) settings

B. Commissioning storage devices

C. Patch management on the EC2 instance's operating system

D. Life-cycle management of IAM credentials

E. Controlling physical access to compute resources

Answer: A, C, D,

OFFICIAL EXPLANATION:

AWS Doc shows the snapshot of the AWS Shared Responsibility Model.

Read More From URL:

https://aws.amazon.com/compliance/shared-responsibility-
model/

266. Mike wants to manage identities in AWS, how can he perform this?

A. AWS MFA

B. AWS TCO

C. AWS IAM

D. AWS Policies

Answer: C

OFFICIAL EXPLANATION:

The AWS Documentation mentions the following AWS Identity and Access Management (IAM) is a web service that helps you securely control access to AWS resources. You use IAM to control who is authenticated (signed in) and authorized (has permissions) to use resources.

Read More From URL:

https://docs.aws.amazon.com/IAM/latest/UserGuide/introduction.html

267. A best practice when working with permissions in AWS is:

A. Ensure the highest privilege access is used

B. Use the root account credentials mostly

C. Use IAM users and groups rarely

D. Ensure the least privilege access is used

Answer: D

OFFICIAL EXPLANATION:

The AWS Documentation mentions the following: When you

create IAM policies, follow the standard security advice of granting least privilege—that is, granting only the permissions required to perform a task. Determine what users need to do and then craft policies for them that let the users perform only those tasks.

Read More From URL:

https://docs.aws.amazon.com/IAM/latest/UserGuide/best-practices.html

268. TTT company wants to enable very fast, easy, and secure transfers of files over long distances between client and Amazon S3 bucket. Can you suggest any one suggestion.

A. FTP

B. HTTP Transfer

C. SNMP

D. Transfer Acceleration

Answer: D

OFFICIAL EXPLANATION:

The AWS Documentation mentions the following Amazon S3 Transfer Acceleration enables fast, easy, and secure transfers of files over long distances between your client and an S3 bucket. Transfer Acceleration takes advantage of Amazon CloudFront's globally distributed edge locations. As the data arrives at an edge location, data is routed to Amazon S3 over an optimized network path.

https://docs.aws.amazon.com/AmazonS3/latest/dev/transfer-acceleration.html

269. Which of the following are attributes which determine the costing of the EC2 Instance. Choose 3 answers from the options given below

A. Instance Type

B. AMI Type

C. Region

D. Corner location

Answer: A, B, C

OFFICIAL EXPLANATION:

If you see the snapshot from the EC2 on-demand pricing page, you can see the different components that make up the pricing

Read More From URL:

https://aws.amazon.com/ec2/pricing/on-demand/

270. For a company low storage cost is paramount, the data is rarely retrieved, and data retrieval times of several hours are acceptable for them. What is the best storage option to use?

A. Aurora

B. AWS Glacier

C. Management console

D. AWS Cloud Watch

Answer: B

OFFICIAL EXPLANATION:

Amazon Glacier is a storage service optimized for infrequently used data, or "cold data" The service provides durable and extremely low-cost storage with security features for data archiving and backup. With Amazon Glacier, you can store your data cost effectively for months, years, or even decades.

Read More From URL:

https://aws.amazon.com/documentation/glacier/

271.Select some of the special features of Amazon S3? Choose 2 answers from the options given below.

A. S3 allows you to store objects of virtually limited size.

B. S3 allows you to store unlimited amounts of data.

C. Objects are directly accessible via a URL

D. Objects are indirectly accessible via a link.

Answer: B, C

OFFICIAL EXPLANATION:

Each object does have a limitation in S3, but you can store virtually unlimited amounts of data Also each object gets a directly accessible URL.

Read More From URL:

https://aws.amazon.com/s3/faqs/

272. A fully managed NoSQL database service that provides fast and predictable performance with seamless scalability is ?

A. AWS EBS Volumes

B. DynamoDB

C. StaticDB

D. MongoDB

Answer: B

OFFICIAL EXPLANATION:

DynamoDB is a fully managed NoSQL offering provided by AWS. It is now available in most regions for users to consume. The link provides the full details on the product.

Read More From URL:

http://docs.aws.amazon.com/amazondynamodb/latest/developer guide/Introduction.html

273. Suppose you want to monitor the CPU utilization of an EC2 resource in AWS. Which of the below services can help in this regard ?

A. AWS Config

B. AWS Cloudwatch

C. AWS Cloud9

D. AWS Cloudformation

Answer: B

OFFICIAL EXPLANATION:

The AWS Documentation mentions the following Amazon CloudWatch is a monitoring service for AWS cloud resources and the applications you run on AWS. You can use Amazon CloudWatch to collect and track metrics, collect and monitor log files, set alarms, and automatically react to changes in your AWS resources. Amazon CloudWatch can monitor AWS resources such as Amazon EC2 instances, Amazon DynamoDB tables, and Amazon RDS DB instances, as well as custom metrics generated by your applications and services, and any log files your applications generate.

Read More From URL:

https://aws.amazon.com/cloudwatch/

274. Which service provides durable storage for static content while utilizing lower Overall CPU resources for the web tier(2- tier application in AWS)?

A. AWS CLI

B. Amazon S3

C. On-Demand instance

D. Management console

Answer: B

OFFICIAL EXPLANATION:

Amazon S3 is the default storage service that should be considered for companies. If provides durable storage for all statiC. content.

Read More From URL:

https://aws.amazon.com/s3/faqs/

275. A company wants distribution of incoming application traffic across multiple EC2 instances, how can they deploy this?

A. AWS ELB

B. AWS EC2

C. AWS EBS Volumes

D. Aurora

Answer: A

OFFICIAL EXPLANATION:

The AWS Documentation mentions the following Elastic Load Balancing distributes incoming application traffic across multiple EC2 instances, in multiple Availability Zones. This increases the fault tolerance of your applications.

Read More From URL:

https://docs.aws.amazon.com/elasticloadbalancing/latest/usergui
de/what-is-load-balancing.html

276. Choose the best option from the below AWS services that
allows you to base the number of resources on the demand of the
application or users.

A. Glacier
B. AWS HDK
C. AWS SDK
D. AWS Autoscaling

Answer: D
OFFICIAL EXPLANATION:
The AWS Documentation mentions the following AWS Auto
Scaling enables you to configure automatic scaling for the scalable
AWS resources for your application in a matter of minutes. AWS
Auto Scaling uses the Auto Scaling and Application Auto Scaling
services to configure scaling policies for your scalable AWS
resources.
Read More From URL:
https://docs.aws.amazon.com/autoscaling/plans/userguide/what-
is-aws-auto-scaling.html

277. An AWS managed database service that provides processing
power that is up to 5X faster than a traditional MySQL database is?

A. Amazon RDS

B. DynamoDB

C. MongoDB

D. Aurora

Answer: D

OFFICIAL EXPLANATION:

The AWS Documentation mentions the following Amazon Aurora (Aurora) is a fully managed, MySQL- and PostgreSQL-compatible, relational database engine. It combines the speed and reliability of high-end commercial databases with the simplicity and cost-effectiveness of open-source databases. It delivers up to five times the throughput of MySQL and up to three times the throughput of PostgreSQL without requiring changes to most of your existing applications.

Read More From URL:

https://docs.aws.amazon.com/AmazonRDS/latest/UserGuide/AuroraOverview.html

278. You want to build a data warehouse on the cloud. Which of the following is AWS services can help?

A. AWS IAM

B. AWS MFA

C. AWS X-RAY

D. AWS Redshift

Answer: D

OFFICIAL EXPLANATION:

The AWS Documentation mentions the following Amazon Redshift is a fully managed, petabyte-scale data warehouse service in the cloud. You can start with just a few hundred gigabytes of data and scale to a petabyte or more. This enables you to use your data to acquire new insights for your business and customers.

Read More From URL:

https://docs.aws.amazon.com/redshift/latest/mgmt/welcome.html

279. The services that helps in governance, compliance, and risk auditing in AWS is?

A. AWS SES

B. AWS Cloudtrail

C. AWS SQS

D. AWS SNS

Answer: B

OFFICIAL EXPLANATION:

The AWS Documentation mentions the following AWS CloudTrail

is a service that enables governance, compliance, operational auditing, and risk auditing of your AWS account. With CloudTrail, you can log, continuously monitor, and retain account activity related to actions across your AWS infrastructure. CloudTrail provides event history of your AWS account activity, including actions taken through the AWS Management Console, AWS SDKs, command line tools, and other AWS services. This event history simplifies security analysis, resource change tracking, and troubleshooting.

Read More From URL:

https://aws.amazon.com/cloudtrail/

280. When using On-Demand instances in AWS, which of the following is NOT TRUE when it comes to the costing for the Instance.

A. You pay no upfront costs for the instance

B. You are charged per second based on the hourly rate

C. You pay for much you use.

D. You have to pay the termination fees if you terminate the instance and also more than what you use

Answer: D

OFFICIAL EXPLANATION:

You don't need to pay any termination fees when it comes to Ec2 Instances

Read More From URL:

https://aws.amazon.com/ec2/pricing/on-demand/

281. What is the use of the storage option known as Amazon Glacier provided by Amazon? Choose any two options

A. Cached continuous data

B. Infrequently accessed data

C. Active cloud base storage

D. Data archives

Answer: B, D

OFFICIAL EXPLANATION:

Amazon Glacier is an extremely low-cost storage service that provides secure, durable, and flexible storage for data backup and archival. So Amazon glacier is used for infrequently accessed data and Data archives.

Read More From URL:

https://aws.amazon.com/glacier/

282. Which database that is not supported in the AWS RDS?

A. Oracle

B. MariaDB

C. Microsoft SQL

D. MongoDB

Answer: D

OFFICIAL EXPLANATION:

MongoDB is NOSQL DB which is not supported in RDS. Amazon RDS is available on several database instance types - optimized for memory, performance or I/O - and provides you with six familiar database engines to choose from, including Amazon Aurora, PostgreSQL, MySQL, MariaDB, Oracle, and Microsoft SQL Server.

Read More From URL:

https://aws.amazon.com/rds/

283. A company wants to move 10 TB data warehouse to the AWS cloud .Which can be used to move this amount of data to the AWS Cloud?

A. Amazon InDirect Connect

B. Amazon Snowball

C. Amazon S3 UniPart Upload

D. Amazon EBS Volumes

Answer: B

OFFICIAL EXPLANATION:

The AWS Documentation mentions the following AWS Snowball

is a service that accelerates transferring large amounts of data into and out of AWS using physical storage appliances, bypassing the Internet. Each AWS Snowball appliance type can transport data at faster-than internet speeds. This transport is done by shipping the data in the appliances through a regional carrier. The appliances are rugged shipping containers, complete with E Ink shipping labels.

Read More From URL:

https://docs.aws.amazon.com/snowball/latest/ug/whatissnowball.html

284. Differentiate between an availability zone and an edge location by choosing any one point?

A. An availability zone is a grouping of AWS resources in a specific region; an edge location is a specific resource within the AWS region

B. Edge locations are not used as control stations for AWS resources

C. An availability zone is an Amazon resource within an AWS region, whereas an edge location will deliver cached content to the closest location to reduce latency

D. An availability zone is an Amazon resource outside an AWS region, whereas an edge location will deliver cached content to the largest location to reduce latency

Answer: C

OFFICIAL EXPLANATION:

In AWS , there are regions with each region separated in a separate geographic area Each region has multiple, isolated locations known as Availability Zones. An availability zone is used to host resources in a specific region.

Read More From URL:

http://docs.aws.amazon.com/AWSEC2/latest/UserGuide/using-regions-availability-zones.html

285. A security feature that is associated with a Subnet in a VPC to protect against Incoming traffic requests is?

A. NACL

B. Public subnet

C. Private subnet

D. AWS Security groups

Answer: A

OFFICIAL EXPLANATION:

The AWS Documentation mentions the following A network access control list (ACL) is an optional layer of security for your VPC. that acts as a firewall for controlling traffic in and out of one or more subnets. You might set up network ACLs with rules similar to your security groups in order to add an additional layer of security to your VPC.

Read More From URL:

https://docs.aws.amazon.com/AmazonVPC/latest/UserGuide/V

PC_ACLs.html

286. XYZ company wants to ensure costs can be reduced if you have multiple accounts, what sort of billing is this?

A. Combined billing

B. Consolidated billing

C. Shared billing

D. It is possible to increase costs with multiple accounts

Answer: B

OFFICIAL EXPLANATION:

You can use the Consolidated Billing feature to consolidate payment for multiple Amazon Web Services (AWS) accounts or multiple Amazon International Services Pvt. Ltd (AISPL) accounts within your organization by designating one of them to be the payer account. With Consolidated Billing, you can see a combined view of AWS charges incurred by all accounts, as well as get a cost report for each individual account associated with your payer account.

Read More From URL:

http://docs.aws.amazon.com/awsaccountbilling/latest/aboutv2/consolidated-billing.html

287. Let's suppose you have a Web application hosted in an EC2 Instance that needs to send notifications based on events. What

service can you get help from?

A. AWS MFA

B. AWS SNS

C. AWS EC2

D. AWS EBS

Answer: B

OFFICIAL EXPLANATION:

The AWS Documentation mentions the following Amazon Simple Notification Service (Amazon SNS) is a web service that enables applications, end-users, and devices to instantly send and receive notifications from the cloud.

Read More From URL:

https://aws.amazon.com/documentation/sns/

288. A document that provides a formal statement of one or more access(permissions) is known as

A. Department

B. Policy

C. Basic

D. Security

Answer: B

OFFICIAL EXPLANATION:

A policy is a JSON document that specifies what a user can do on AWS. This document consists of • Actions: what actions you will allow. Each AWS service has its own set of actions. • Resources: which resources you allow the action on. • Effect: what the effect will be when the user requests access—either allow or deny. The AWS Documentation mentions the following A policy is an entity in AWS that, when attached to an identity or resource, defines their permissions. AWS evaluates these policies when a principal, such as a user, makes a request. Permissions in the policies determine whether the request is allowed or denied

Read More From URL:

https://docs.aws.amazon.com/IAM/latest/UserGuide/access_pol icies.html

289. I want to control the traffic allowed to reach one or more instances by using any one of the below firewall services. Which can I make use of?

A. Policy

B. NACL

C. CLI

D. Security group

Answer: D

OFFICIAL EXPLANATION:

A security group acts as a virtual firewall for your instance to control inbound and outbound traffic When you launch an instance in a VPC, you can assign the instance to up to five security groups. Security groups act at the instance level. Below is an example of a security group which has inbound rules. The below rule states that users can only SSH into EC2 instances that are attached to this security group.

Read More From URL:

https://docs.aws.amazon.com/AmazonVPC/latest/UserGuide/VPC_SecurityGroups.html

290. What are the advantages of the AWS's Relational Database Service (RDS)? Choose the 2 correct options

A. Automated patches and backups
B. You can resize the capacity accordingly
C. Cannot resize the capacity
D. manual patches and backups

Answer: A, B

OFFICIAL EXPLANATION:

The AWS Documentation mentions the following Amazon Relational Database Service (Amazon RDS) makes it easy to set up, operate, and scale a relational database in the cloud It provides cost-efficient and resizable capacity while automating time-consuming administration tasks such as hardware provisioning, database setup, patching and backups. It frees you to focus on your applications so you can give them the fast performance, high availability, security and compatibility they need

Read More From URL:

https://aws.amazon.com/rds/

291. Mark is using Edge Locations for content caching, how can he do it?

A. AWS SQS

B. AWS CloudFormation

C. AWS Cloudfront

D. AWS Cloud9

Answer: C

OFFICIAL EXPLANATION:

The AWS Documentation mentions the following Amazon CloudFront employs a global network of edge locations and regional edge caches that cache copies of your content close to your viewers. Amazon CloudFront ensures that end-user requests are served by the closest edge location.

Read More From URL:

https://aws.amazon.com/cloudfront/details/

292. Which AWS service can be used to create standard templates for deployment of the Infrastructure.

A. Amazon S3

B. AWS EBS volumes

C. AWS CLI

D. AWS CloudFormation

Answer: D

OFFICIAL EXPLANATION:

AWS CloudFormation gives developers and systems administrators an easy way to create and manage a collection of related AWS resources, provisioning and updating them in an orderly and predictable fashion.

Read More From URL:

https://aws.amazon.com/cloudformation/

293. You have an application that is designed to recover gracefully from Amazon EC2 instance failures in the most cost-effective way. Which of the following will meet your requirements?

A. No upfront reserved instances

B. Spot Instances

C. Partial upfront reserved instances

D. Dedicated instances

Answer: B

OFFICIAL EXPLANATION:

When you think of cost effectiveness, you can either have to choose Spot or Reserved instances. Now when you have a regular processing job, the best is to use spot instances and since your application is designed recover gracefully from Amazon EC2 instance failures, then even if you lose the Spot instance, there is no issue because your application can recover.

Read More From URL:

https://aws.amazon.com/ec2/spot/

294. The AWS service that lets you host Domain Name systems is known as?

A. Route 53

B. IAM

C. InDirect Connect

D. Route 54

Answer: A

OFFICIAL EXPLANATION:

Amazon Route 53 provides highly available and scalable Domain Name System (DNS), domain name registration, and health-checking web services. It is designed to give developers and businesses an extremely reliable and cost effective way to route end users to Internet applications by translating names like example.com into the numeric IP addresses, such as 192.0.2.1, that computers use to connect to each other.

Read More From URL:

https://aws.amazon.com/route53/faqs/

295. The AWS service that allows developers to easily deploy and manage applications on the cloud is called as?

A. CloudWatch

B. Elastic Beanstalk

C. DevOpswork

D. Cloud Config

Answer: B

OFFICIAL EXPLANATION:

AWS Elastic Beanstalk makes it even easier for developers to quickly deploy and manage applications in the AWS Cloud Developers simply upload their application, and Elastic Beanstalk automatically handles the deployment details of capacity provisioning, load balancing, auto-scaling, and application health monitoring.

Read More From URL:

https://aws.amazon.com/elasticbeanstalk/faqs/

296. A company wants to store their most frequently used data so that the response time for the application is improved. Which AWS service provides the solution for the company's requirements?

A. Microsoft SQL Installed on two Amazon EC2 Instances in two Availability Zones.

B. Amazon RDS for MySQL with One-AZ

C. Amazon ElastiCache

D. Amazon MariaDB

Answer: C

OFFICIAL EXPLANATION:

Amazon ElastiCache is a web service that makes it easy to deploy, operate, and scale an in-memory data store or cache in the cloud The service improves the performance of web applications by allowing you to retrieve information from fast, managed, in-memory data stores, instead of relying entirely on slower disk-based databases.

Read More From URL:

https://aws.amazon.com/elasticache/

297. What would you do if you wanted to take a backup of an EBS Volume?

A. Create an EBS snapshot

B. Delete an EBS Snapshot

C. Store the EBS volume in Aurora

D. Store the EBS volume in StaticDB

Answer: A

OFFICIAL EXPLANATION:

The AWS Documentation mentions the following You can back up the data on your Amazon EBS volumes to Amazon S3 by taking point-in-time snapshots.

Read More From URL:

https://docs.aws.amazon.com/AWSEC2/latest/UserGuide/EBSS napshots.html

298. Choose the services that Amazon EC2 provides.

A. Virtual servers in the Cloud

B. Many platforms to run code (Java, PHP, Python), paying on an hourly basis.

C. Real servers in the cloud

D. Physical servers, remotely managed by the computer

Answer: A

OFFICIAL EXPLANATION:

Amazon Elastic Compute Cloud (Amazon EC2) is a web service that provides resizable compute capacity in the cloud It is designed to make web-scale cloud computing easier for developers. Amazon EC2's simple web service interface allows you to obtain and configure capacity with minimal friction. It provides you with complete control of your computing resources and lets you run on Amazon's proven computing environment. Amazon EC2 reduces the time required to obtain and boot new server instances to minutes, allowing you to quickly scale capacity, both up and down, as your computing requirements change.

Read More From URL:

https://aws.amazon.com/ec2/

299. AWS RDS allows for AWS to failover to a secondary database in case the primary one fails. Justify the statement by selecting any one option.

A. AWS Multi-AZ

B. AWS Failagain

C. AWS Primary

D. AWS Single-AZ

Answer: A

OFFICIAL EXPLANATION:

The AWS Documentation mentions the following Amazon RDS Multi-AZ deployments provide enhanced availability and durability for Database (DB) Instances, making them a natural fit for production database workloads. When you provision a Multi-AZ DB Instance, Amazon RDS automatically creates a primary DB Instance and synchronously replicates the data to a standby instance in a different Availability Zone (AZ). Each AZ runs on its own physically distinct, independent infrastructure, and is engineered to be highly reliable. In case of an infrastructure failure,

Amazon RDS performs an automatic failover to the standby (or to a read replica in the case of Amazon Aurora), so that you can resume database operations as soon as the failover is complete.

Read More From URL:

https://aws.amazon.com/rds/details/multi-az/

300. A company wants to manage the costs for all resources in AWS. How can they do it?

A. AWS Billing

B. Management console

C. Cost Explorer

D. Transaction history

Answer: C

OFFICIAL EXPLANATION:

The AWS Documentation mentions the following Cost Explorer is a free tool that you can use to view your costs. You can view your costs as either a cash-based view (costs are recorded when cash is received or paid) with unblended costs or as an accrual-based view (costs are recorded when income is earned or costs are incurred). You can view data for up to the last 13 months, forecast how much you are likely to spend for the next three months, and get recommendations for what Reserved Instances to purchase

Read More From URL:

https://docs.aws.amazon.com/awsaccountbilling/latest/aboutv2/cost-explorer-what-is.html

Thank You
All The best

We have taken care in preparing each question in the book., in spite of it if there are corrections to be made in the book please feel free to mail us at care@bigbangtechno.in . Our Architect will validate it and make the corresponding changes. After the changes are made, **we will publish your name with a 'Vote of Thanks' in Amazon Kindle Book Publish website.**

We hope you are satisfied with this book. **If you feel this book has helped you in some way for your preparation, please rate us 5 star in Amazon Kindle.** It will be a great moral support to us and will help us to improve the quality of the book in the forthcoming editions.

Made in the USA
Monee, IL
09 August 2021